Pecked To Death By Goslings

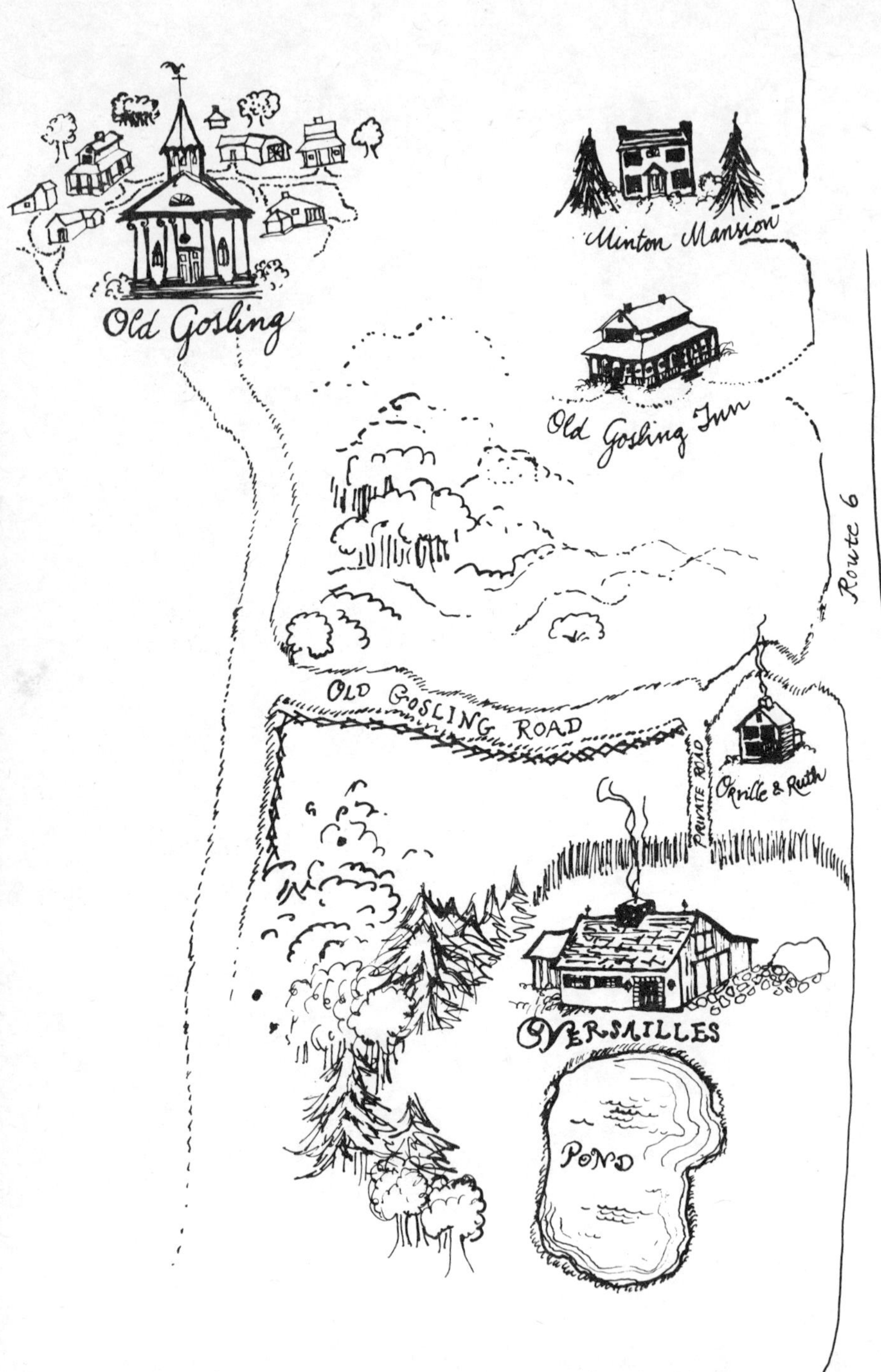
Old Gosling
Minton Mansion
Old Gosling Inn
Route 6
OLD GOSLING ROAD
PRIVATE ROAD
Orville & Ruth
VERSAILLES
POND

PECKED TO DEATH BY GOSLINGS

By Jane Trahey

Prentice-Hall, Inc., Englewood Cliffs, New Jersey

For Anita Richter . . .
my only and adorable sister,
who tagged the barn
"Spider Heaven" . . .
with love

Also by Jane Trahey

Taste of Texas
The Magic Yarn
Life with Mother Superior
100 Years of Harper's Bazaar

Co-author

Complete Martini Cookbook
Son of Martini Cookbook
1000 Names and Where to Drop Them

Pecked To Death By Goslings

Seventy-five cents is one hell of a lot of money for the Sunday *New York Times,* but if that's what it costs to keep in touch with the outside world, you pays your money and you keeps your mouth shut. Why, in Marlboro country where I lived, well over a hundred people plunked down three quarters every Wednesday (when the Sunday *Times* arrived) just to see what we weren't ever going to see. The truly wealthy Marlborians, who could have bought *The New York Times* lock, stock, and Sulzbergers, paid $1.50 for it to come by air.

We all lived from week to week on handouts from the big-city newspaper. It was an incredibly masochistic thing to do. We'd absolutely crow with excitement about any new hot play, knowing full well that that very week we'd have a local tour of *Medea* with stars like Ethel Merman and Jack Carson. But it wasn't only show biz that turned us provincials on and made us green with envy. From Hammacher Schlemmer to the Museum of Modern Art, if "it" was "it," "it" was *there.*

Every year, whenever I got that wild-hungry-got-to-split feeling, I would send out a batch of letters to the big city. Each year Madison Avenue made it clear that they didn't need anyone to help out, particularly that they didn't need anything female. After several hundred letters, I decided that I couldn't possibly starve harder if I simply started an advertising agency. As my father the fighter always said, "If you can't lick 'em, join 'em."

It may sound simple, but it's a long trip from Downtown Nowhere to Uptown Gotham. But that was where I wanted to be. I hummed a lot my very first spring in the beautiful big city as I walked over subway grates and smelled the fetid air of a thousand trains going somewhere. Papers, broken bottles, garbage of great assortment was underfoot, but I vastly preferred it to Mama's ferns and arsenic spray.

My bedroom, on the East Side of Manhattan on Sixty-first Street, was encased in a one-hundred-year-old brownstone. I had the exotic smell of the Italian restaurant's garlic buds which were dropped by the thousands into hot grease every morning at eight. It was better than any azalea, camellia, pecan or praline I had ever smelled. Two of America's hottest department stores were in my backyard, and a cute rat lived in my basement. For my money it was hog heaven.

It wasn't until Memorial Day—in fact, it was the eve of the thirtieth of May—that the first dissonant note in my City Symphony was sounded. I found out that the Summer Festival was definitely not on the agenda of the native New Yorker. The New Yorker has a disease that strikes him each Thursday evening, hits hardest on Friday morning, and keeps him out of city environs until Sunday night, like the three-day flu bug. Dum-Dum me didn't have an inkling of this virus. Since I had nowhere to go but home to my new "just-won" haven in the Sixties, there seemed little need for me to grab a suitcase and light out early from the office. Why on earth would anyone in his right mind want to leave the city?

I soon found out.

On weekends, the streets were empty, there were no cabs, no traffic, no shops open, no galleries, not even a whiff of garlic. The good butcher was gone, and the theaters were filled with busloads of Jerseyites who had bought up all the tickets to the hot shows. The people I came in contact with were the summer replacements for the regular citizens, and the only people who stayed were the disgruntled and the deprived.

All my friends vanished. I ate alone. I watched summer replacement for Saturday night TV. The building I lived in was as quiet as a funeral home without a body.

By the end of June, I was getting a bit lonely in Fun City. Though I was content in my garden of cement and loathe to ever leave it, there wasn't one Adam or Eve to talk to. Even answering services weren't answering.

The Monday before the Fourth of July, I lunched out with a pal, Peter Carpenter. Peter was a successful book agent who had come to New York a few years earlier than I. Under all his paraphernalia of Meledandri suits, wide ties, pajama-top shirts, and long hair, there beat the heart of a Midwesterner, and I knew I could level with him. I simply, bluntly, asked him what went on every weekend.

"Where does everyone go on Friday night?"

"You stay here on weekends? My God!" he said, looking amazed, dumbfounded, and sad, as if he had come into my cold, snow-filled room on Christmas to see me with pneumonia and an empty larder.

"Oh, I'm not complaining," I said, trying to sound cheery. "I just wondered. I love the city and I've had a good chance to really see it. But it's not much fun always being alone."

"Well, we'll do something about it right away. I had no idea you had no place to go or no invites." Sunburned and smiling, he got out his little black book and headed for the phone.

Returning, he slipped into the booth next to me and said, "Okay, you're fixed. You'll come with me to the Cranwells this weekend. You know both Emma and Bruce, and they have a great pad in Montauk. You'll have to take the daybed, but my God, *anything* is better than the four days here in New York!"

And so I finally became a true New Yorker. My qualifications were complete. I had come from out-of-town to live in an apartment instead of a house (the apartment cost more than the whole house). I was earning considerably less doing the same work I had done in Marlboro. I wrote glowing letters home about the city because at last I felt that sense of upsmanship that they were on the outside and I was on the "in." Now I could add the final touch: I would be able to say, "I spend my weekends in Bucks or Sag Harbor or Fire Island or Connecticut." My cycle was complete. Real New Yorkers leave New York after they arrive.

So never mind when I *should* have left for Montauk to visit the Cranwells for that gorgeous Fourth of July weekend. I *should* have left on Thursday morning, just to get to Penn Station. I waited till it was Friday afternoon and raining. All cabs had long since gone to Valhalla. I was soaked by the time I finally killed a little old lady to get one. Penn Station looked like a nuclear alert had gone out and all the citizens were beating it. I raced over to the Information window. Thirty-seven fat children, in line with their captain on their way to Fat Camp, had definite priority. By the time I found out where the train was, I had missed it. The ticket man was helpful when I asked him if there was another way to get to Montauk. He said, "You should have caught the 4:37." Rebellion welled up in me. Maybe I should have quit and gone to Fat Camp.

I phoned Peter at the Cranwells.

"Oh, poor darling, you're jinxed. I should have made you leave with us yesterday. Well, you could drive down, but I don't think you'd be able to rent a car now on such short notice. Wait a minute," Peter said, putting his hand over the mouthpiece. The phone booth was unbearably hot and sticky, and the mob that had offered to burn me at the Information Center were now lined up with torches at the phone booth. "Emma says there's a bus, but it gets in at midnight. She thinks you ought to fly. There's a little taxi plane at Twenty-third Street. See if you can get on it tomorrow, and we'll pick you up at the Montauk Club. It comes in there."

"I'll find out and call you back."

I wrung out my dress when I got back home. The apartment was cool, calm, and deadly quiet. I called the taxi-plane service, and they said they'd take me. I mixed a drink and channeled in on summer-replacement TV for Friday night. My God, even with an invitation strangled out of the poor Cranwells, I was back in my cell. The fact that I was calling my dream "the cell" prompted more ice cubes and more gin. Could it be that the cement was not greener on the other side?

At 8 A.M. it was so hot you could watch the air shimmer. I hungered for the sea breezes, for the lap of the ocean, for the sun on my nose, for a cool breath of fresh air. I arrived at the cement air wharf that was also a filling station. I boarded a plane that resembled a Campbell's soup can perched on toothpicks stuck in two slabs of cheese. The pilot shut the door and zipped out the only air in the world. We taxied down the East River, turned around at the United Nations Building, and water-skiied back to the filling-station ticket office. We did this three times. On the last trip, the pilot apologized. "Sorry, can't lift her. Not enough air."

Well, there went my sandy pebbles and the blue Atlantic. I was so mad I abandoned my savings, went to the regular airport, and chartered a private plane. I arrived in Southhampton at 5 P.M. With luck and a ten-dollar taxi ride, I made it to Montauk for the sunset.

Pete and the Cranwells were well into cocktails. (For the record, they were stoned out of their cotton-pickin' heads.) Naturally, it was partially my fault, since they had postponed lunch at Montauk Harbor Club till four o'clock. Then, assured of my death at sea, they had finished up seventeen Bloody Marys and switched to martinis which, they said, "didn't tasht so tomato-ey."

While I tried to clean up in a sadly run-down john —which, I might add, would not get a star at Texaco —Emma shouted to me the primary rules of the house.

"Dear, can you hear me?" This was funny, actually, since only a sheet of Japanese rice paper separated me from anyone in the place.

"Yes, I can hear you fine."

"Oh, good. Well, what I was going to say was please don't put Kleenex in the toilet; it backs up. And wait till the motor stops pumping before you flush . . . Okay?"

She went away and then returned with this palatable afterthought. "In fact, dear, don't put anything down the toilet."

Since I was the last invited guest, I got the daybed, as forewarned. And the daybed was an integral part of the social life of the Cranwells, since their Castro occupied most of the living room. During the day it was covered by a damp Baggie, and at night, I soon found out, it had a matching personality of damp sheets and a damp mattress with lumps that went bang in the night.

As we watched the final light fade over the deep-blue Atlantic, I studied the house that the Cranwells had for the season—and at no mean rent, I was quickly made to understand. I tried to apply the rules of logic: "All houses have walls, roofs, windows, doors, and floors; this has walls, roofs, windows, doors, and floors. Therefore, this is a house." But the syllogism didn't work. This "house" should have been demolished. I kept thinking that if the Cranwells would only grow potatoes, the government would surely give them a poverty loan.

Actually I had never seen an all-linoleum house before. The floor was linoleum; the table was covered with a dew-crested linoleum; the toilet seat was linoleum. Moreover, the shower was wet before you ran the water, and the Calvin Coolidge furniture was wet. How could the swinging Cranwells, who owned an art gallery and lived on posh Sutton Place in a Billy-Baldwin-decorated apartment, put up their bucks for this horror house? I kept thinking about my nice, lonely, quiet apartment and Saturday night television. No TV could have survived in this house without being grounded.

My hands were sticky, my face clammy, and my feet cold. My hair went limp the second I hit their dune-grass patio, so I looked like a borzoi in a high wind. But I did have one day in the sun and sand.

On Monday, Pete suggested we leave right after

breakfast. "On a holiday like this, it's traffic all the way if we don't."

It was traffic all the way when we did. Bumper to bumper, we crawled along the Long Island Expressway for four hours. If one more time in my life I hear someone say, "Montauk? Why it's nothing. We do it in two hours," I'll crack them right in the mouth. They are either lying or flying. After all, just remember the next stop after Montauk *is* Portugal.

For my next weekend away from Mecca, Peter's good friend Jeannie gave me his weekend invitation while he flew to Paris. What luck. It was my first look at Never Find It Lake. Jeannie shared this pad with two otherwise gentle, well-mannered, well-dressed, fashion-hip women. "It's just old shoe," Jeannie warned. "You know, rustic, real country. We like to get away from all the chic and stuff."

Well, when this team got away from it all, they really left the ground. They had reverted completely to basic pioneer. They adored swimming in slimy Never Find It Lake. They chopped their own firewood. The only usable water came from a large hand pump in the yard. I was considered quite gauche when I mentioned their Paleolithic toilet. When I had been invited, I was told, "Just bring shorts and shirts and pants. No one needs a dress here." Since the place was just one step short of *Lord of the Flies,* anything worn was merely protection against total insect poisoning.

Like a fool, I had failed to bring a few simple survival items: a gallon of Raid, a spray gun, a machine gun, a stick of considerable size, a large tin of 6-12 to keep the tsetses off me, and calamine lotion for those that got through my constant paper-waving.

The cottage was pure Abe Lincoln. Since the logs were not tuck-pointed, there was little point to the screens in the windows. The bugs intelligently sifted through the logs. Instead of electricity there were those cute little wheezing inventions called Coleman Lanterns. My room had been converted from a closet. It had one window, and I quickly discovered that whereas the shade wouldn't stay down, the window wouldn't stay up.

I couldn't sleep worth a damn. The mosquitoes whined *over* my head. There were things *under* my head. And the most incredible racket pounded on the roof just *above* my head. Dawn finally came. Just as I fell asleep with two mosquito wings between my index finger and thumb, Betty, the most civilized of the trio, flew into my room with a pitcher of tepid water. I opened the slits of my swollen, bitten eyes and could have sworn she had on a full length graywool Pilgrim outfit.

"Here, sissy," the Puritan shouted, her coveredwagon smile lording it over me. "I've heated some water for you so you won't start griping. But," she added, "this is it. I'm not going to spoil you all weekend."

"What was that sound on the roof? Like hail. Didn't you hear it?"

"Oh, that. Squirrels playing, or maybe water rats."

I fainted. "Water rats," I mumbled when I came to. "How too cute."

This seemed to cheer her, so she went out to hack up the forest for wood to heat coffee. "We rinse at the pump," she piped.

I was an absolute delight at the well. Every time I got to the point where I needed water, the pump finked out and had to be primed. I did my toilette with a white foaming mouth, and when I finally stopped gagging, I had solid dry teeth and soaked feet.

"Don't you just love well water?" asked the trio cheerfully.

"No."

This was wrong and I knew it. Negativeness was never going to get me anywhere. Nor could I go anywhere without a car, and I couldn't get out until the driver wanted out. Though it had been a mistake to drive up with them, I had made mental notes on the original directions they had given me. Had I followed them, I would never have been lucky enough to find Never Find It Lake.

I could kid myself just so long. Sooner or later I had to use "those" facilities. The Chick Sales department was simply not for me. I devised a complicated plan to outfox the whole lot of them: borrow the car, tell them I had to buy a paper, and use any filling station within the county. I got the car out of them three times that day, but I was down to buying *Boy's Life* at the paper store and the Shell man thought I had a car fetish.

Never End It Weekend terminated at 1:30 A.M. "We always leave late to avoid the traffic on the Taconic." Finally, I was deposited in front of my door. I dragged my mosquito-riddled unwashed body up the steps. I turned on my air conditioner and a summer replacement for the Late Late Late Show. I bathed in bath oil, applied lotion to my bug-pecked legs, opened a split of champagne, and flushed the toilet for the sheer hell of it.

I was home, home, home and until the next Friday I was safe.

At last Labor Day came: the high holiday of the entire summer, the Yom Kippur of weekends. There is a touch of sadness about it, for it marks the end of the thirty-two-hour week, the end of the good life, the relaxed psyche, and the tanned body.

This glorious holiday started when I crushed my way on to a train for Jamaica, where I caught another train to a designated spot to meet Kit and Bob in their vintage Volkswagen. (This was done to avoid traffic and bring on my first stroke.) A lot of people claim that you can't guess the age of a Volkswagen. I'll tell you how: If your Warner's bra can't take the bouncing, it's an old, old one. Bob's car must have been twenty-five years old and been used at the bombing of Stuttgart. We flew in and out and up and down rutty back roads. Bob is a traffic pilot and had obviously marked every unused road in the county. The goal was a beach house fondly tagged "The Mouse House."

It had a dune floor, and no shades at all, and the

furniture had been left by the previous tenants—
the mice. All of it was driftwood by origin. My bedside table was a drifting piece of driftwood, several
pornographic driftwoods hung on walls, and my bed's
headboard was a dangerous reef of driftwood. The
lamp, well, I needn't tell you about that lamp.

Since guests can't be hosts, I had been sharing my
bedside tables with other guests all summer. When
I woke up this glorious first day of Labor Day weekend in a beach house on the Island in the township
of Quoquay, I counted thirty-three glasses of old
bourbon and old Scotch. Some lipsticked glasses had
cocktail onions still floating in the bottom, rather
like my eyeballs.

It was seven o'clock and I wondered momentarily
why I was up. Then I heard the machinery going full
blast. The homey, charming, fun farmer next door
was running his threshing machine.

"My God! How do you stand the noise?" There I
went again, complaining about the ambience.

"We never hear it anymore; I guess we're used
to it."

The thought must have struck Kit at the same moment it did me. How come they were up at 7 A.M.,
too, if they were used to it?

"You wouldn't want to spend this beautiful day in
bed, would you?"

Like any good guest, I lied. "No, of course not."
But what I really meant was, "Yes, I'd adore to."

The major effort for Sunday was a clambake. A
handsome, tall, bronzed god seemed to be in charge.

From the way he talked and ordered us around, I knew he came from a fishing fleet in Gloucester run by his old granddaddy who wore a black slicker and caught lobsters for a living. His directions were quite explicit: we had to dig a hole in the sand big enough for a body, gather great stones, lay them in to heat, and cover them with layers and layers of seaweed.

After seven rounds of something called "Virgin's Downfall," it became imperative to keep the fire burning and keep people from becoming tinder. We barely caught one fat, rather stoned lady who was hell-bent on making a funeral pyre of herself and ruining the lobsters. By eleven o'clock the still-pink chickens would have appealed only to a fancier of chicken tartar. The lobsters were barely coming along in their boiling garbage cans. Kit, in an effort to survive, finally got several of the men to tote all the food to the house stove away from Gloucester's pyre. It was then I learned that our Calvin Clambake was from Waxahachie, Texas, where lobster was unheard of.

"I'll be damned if I know what went wrong, Bob." Calvin stuttered now from the cold. "I read them directions in the *TV Guide,* and it sounded simple as hell."

During the summer I had learned the fine distinction between the haves and have-nots, the hosts and the guests. Chatty little articles popped up in *McCall's* and *Vogue* and *Bazaar* that gave very definite instructions on how to behave as a guest: what to bring your host, what to send your hostess. What these articles flagrantly left out was what the Host should do for me.

If nothing else, minimum wages were in order. The host, it became obvious to me, made the minor investment of renting or buying a house and supplying it with the barest essentials. Then, instead of hiring coolie labor, he invited guests.

I made a list of what I had accomplished that summer on just a few weekends. I had made beds, folded sheets, folded beds, shopped, toted, treated, carried, cooked, washed, trimmed, sanded, sprayed, painted, cut, and weeded. Painting was actually my specialty, and I did several sets of wicker chairs that would have cost mine host at least one hundred bucks.

I say nothing of my Diner's bills, for it was only decent to either pop for lunch or dinner on a weekend or spend $25 buying gourmet cheeses and wine. If I had gotten Schrafft's rate for my kitchen labors, I would have earned at least $46.75 with benefits. But for the average cost to me per weekend, including fares, I could have stayed in a suite at the Plaza and had room service.

Fall never looked so enticing to me. If weekends were what I had experienced, thank heaven the summer had come to a close. I knew what had to be done: If I was to live through another summer without being a true loner in Gotham, I would have to find a place of my own. Maybe I could turn up a place that was pretty, like Marlboro country, like Mama's house. At least *I* could call the shots, shop when I felt like shopping, bathe when I felt like bathing, eat what I wanted, have my own driftwood, and my own canapés on it.

Next summer, I vowed, would be different.

II

Lord knows, I thought, there can't be anything very difficult about buying an existing house. My first and last venture into building had been in conjunction with an insane architect in Marlboro country—a modern house that caused no small amount of comment from my neighbors. The census taker had actually asked if it was going to be used for a dwelling. No more glass that leaked and redwood that creaked! My next house would be old, restored, worn, and private. I had only to find a charming, well-built, small eighteenth-century, completely-fixed-up house, with a backyard in the country and a front yard in the ocean. Cheap.

It's so easy when you know exactly what you want. That fall I looked at about 2,700 houses.

If a house had enough bedrooms, it had no fireplace. If it was a plan of perfection, it had no hot water or fronted on Mosquito Junction. If it was easily accessible, so were fifty neighbors right smack in the middle of their own population explosion.

I saw a dear place on the Housatonic River, but it was right next door to a motor-boat school. The old Jane Eyre house I loved in Bucks County had a path that Girl Scouts used for their leaf tours. Behind a perfect Hampton beach house lurked a nightclub that attracted a very odd crowd Saturday nights.

Candlewood Lake was fine, except the houses had to be brown and trimmed with red.

Breadfruit Farm was a delight, but the agent made it clear that people living there had to like their neighbors.

Clam Bay restricted people.

And then one Sunday I read that ad in the *Times*. It appealed to me. "It" was located in Old Gosling, the third oldest town in all of Connecticut, just three miles from the Sound. The town boasts an 1781 Presbyterian Church with lighted spires after seven. A Main Street with 150-year-old elms and three gas stations all closed on Sunday nights. Old Gosling would most certainly stir up my American heritage, if nothing else. And—this was the best of all—it was only sixty miles from the megalopolis.

> 16½ acres of lovely wooded property,
> with a farmhouse and barn. Large pond
> on property. Near School.

I didn't need the school but the rest sounded great. I called the number and a deep masculine voice answered my various questions.

"Yep, the house has plumbing."

"Yep, it's turn-of-the-century."

"Nope, the barn is not restored."

Yep, I could see it that very day. I picked up the masculine voice at the real-estate agent's home. She was a good seventy, had frizzy, applesaucey hair that was bright red, and she smoked cigars—not Tiparillos.

"My name is Ma Henderson." She puffed her cheroot and studied me as thoroughly as I have ever been studied. "Want one?" She offered me a big black cigar.

"No," I said sheepishly, fearing to offend her. "I don't smoke. I only engage in the major vices." I hoped this might salvage my personality.

"Eh, eh, eh." It was a rare laugh. "That's pretty good, girl, but I'm here to tell you, once you enjoy a good cigar, you won't want nothing else. C'mon, let's go."

We hopped into her vintage car and off we flew. Up rutty roads, careening around forks, over the meadows, and down through the vales. I was petrified.

Then I saw it. It was at the very end of a long rutty path. An old dilapidated barn. Bright green and bright yellow, about half and half, like the last farmer had some leftover paint and wanted to use it all up.

"I thought you said it had a farmhouse."

"Sold it this morning."

"Oh, damn," I said. "I don't think there's much I could do with this."

"Sold the house to a nice couple. Now I have just the sixteen acres and the pond and this here barn."

"Well, I most certainly couldn't live in this."

"Why, you most certainly could. Why, it's all the vogue to fix up old barns, didn't you know that?"

I followed the lure. "Well, I guess it won't hurt to look."

We went through the barn. The bottom floor was pitch-black and muddy.

"Here's where the chickens stayed. Cock-a-doodle-dooooo," she crowed. "Cock-a-doooodle-doooooo."

For a brief second I felt like bolting up the steps, and if I had, it would have been the smartest bolt I ever made. She pushed aside several big tanks and pulled me by the hand through a rusty web of chicken wire on the mud floor.

"Hoooooooooooooieeeeeee. Hooooooooeeeeeeeee. Hoooieeeee," she hooied at the top of her lungs.

"Pigs?" I said, pleased as an idiot who had guessed correctly and won a pony ride.

"Good girl."

It seemed that now Ma and I would have communication only in farm sounds. What in the name of heaven was I doing in the cellar of an old barn with this crazy old cigar-smoking witch shouting out pig latin? And, what's more, why was I delighted at having guessed her pig call as a pig?

We followed the trough to the end of the building. Then Ma Henderson began to whinny all the way back to the pasture doors. But there was an aching sensation in my stomach that this could indeed be a big fat house.

The pond was idyllic, with a huge old turtle sunning himself on the rock. He was about the size of Ma Henderson's Ford and might well have been a prop because I've never laid eyes on him since.

The surrounding woods were dappled with sunlight. The meadow with the barn facing it could most certainly be a yard. I honestly didn't think it could cost a whale of a lot to put in a bathroom and a floor. That's all I figured it would need.

Ma Henderson was not in business for nothing.

"Let you have the whole kit and caboodle for sixteen."

As I recalled, I had lost a farmhouse somewhere.

"There's still sixteen acres, and up hereabouts, land is worth nearly a thousand an acre. Why, the barn's a present, that's what."

"Let me look around again."

"Go right ahead, but you had better take it if you have any feeling for it, 'cause it won't be here next Sunday. A buy like this is bound to be snapped up. Of course," she added, lighting a new cigar, "you'd have to know what to do with it. Person with the right imagination could pull it off, turn it to a palace, but the wrong person would be in deep trouble. But then, a wrong person wouldn't see its potential anyway, not in a trillion years, they wouldn't."

It was like telling Richard Nixon he'd never be President.

"I sure know what I'd like to do with it."

"Well, you're the first one come up here that I'd put a dime on."

I rose to the bait. I let her place it in my mouth as she tugged expertly. "Okay," I said, "let me give you some holding money till I get to the bank."

"It's a deal." She was so enchanted she made a smoke ring and poked her finger in the middle of it.

I fretted like any potential poorhouse inmate all

week. Was it the right thing? Was it possible? Would renovation cost a fortune? Who'd do it? I was a sucker, she was a fiend.

The following Sunday I bought it. The following Thursday I went to the closing, and the barn was mine.

"Who bought the farmhouse, really, Mrs. Henderson?"

"Lovely couple. Nice couple. Just beat you by a minute, too. Family is from Old Gosling. You'll like them. They're far enough away not to bother you. You won't ever see them."

And then I went to Town Hall to see if they could dig up any old surveys of the land.

"Hear you bought just the barn?" the clerk asked, as he dug through his files.

"Yes, do you know the property?"

"Sure do. How come you didn't take the whole package?"

"Just before I got there, Ma Henderson had sold the farmhouse."

"You don't say?"

"I do say."

"You know who bought that piece of property?" He peered at me over the counter.

"Nice old couple," I babbled, imitating Ma Henderson. "Old Gosling, so I'm told."

"Well, I'm going to let you in on a little secret, lady. I'm going to tell you who bought that piece. Ma Henderson did. She bought it *after* you bought yours. The day after, and she bought it for her son, Orville, and his wife and family. That's quite a family Orville's got. Ten children now. Yep, ten. Beautiful children, too."

That conniving, cigar-smoking, Swamp Yankee peddler had used *my* down payment to buy the farmhouse! "Ten children's a lot," I mumbled. At least it was true that I couldn't see the farmhouse from the barn—it was behind a knoll. But, let me tell you, the people in the farmhouse could certainly see me.

But as I console myself now, if it hadn't been for Ma Henderson and Orville and Orville's wife and their ten I would never have had Clovis.

III

The day the contractor agreed to meet me was the day I met Orville, Orville's wife, and the Big Ten. They came over to watch. They didn't talk much—the other eleven, that is. It was Orville who was the big mouth.

Mrs. Henderson was called Ruthie, an odd name for an Eskimo, which is what she was. "Pure Chukchi," Orville boasted. Ruthie was quite pleasant, grunted a lot, and was very, very pregnant. From that first meeting, whenever I arrived they were there, as if the lead dogsled had alerted them that I was on my way. They didn't stay long; they just gave me a good staring over and left. And Ruthie usually brought a piece of jerked beef (her specialty), a slice of caribou that Orville had caught, or a tomato plant. But as I soon realized, Orville was the problem.

He was a tiny, wizened man who was only in his forties but he looked sixty-five. His one bid for fame had come when he served as a Commando trainer in the Aleutian Islands. (Obviously that's where he tackled Ruthie.) But while Ruthie had adjusted to civilization somewhat, Orville never forgot his Commando training. He still approached everyone and everything with an imaginary knife in his teeth and sneakers on his feet.

I found that out on the biggest Sunday of National

Wasp Month, I was knocking down a few nests and spraying them as quickly as I could with Black Flag. If any of the wasps chased me, which was almost constantly, I ran into the woods as fast as my sneakers could go. Now it was a real game for Orville to pop out from behind a bush or a rock and grab me by the shoulder just as he must have done to the enemy.

The first time it happened, I almost fainted from shock and fear. Orville had to get me a glass of soda pop to relieve my hysteria and hiccups, and with him around I had plenty of both. I tried to get Ruthie to understand that it wasn't cricket for him to jump out from behind anything. I just didn't need it, I said, after a week in the city.

"Oh, pay no 'tention to Orville. He scare us, too." That was Ruthie's contribution.

I made up my mind that Orville wasn't going to get me again. To keep him out, I fenced the road at considerable expense, spending money I would rather have put into the house. But it was that or the booby hatch—or an Army training center. I hoped the Hendersons would take the hint. After all, what else could eight feet of wood planks mean? Well, here's what it meant. It meant that Ruthie came through the gate with her brood and the strawberries or raw fish. And Orville, to show his ken at the high jump, simply flew over it, much to the high enjoyment of his four littlest. He was okay at dawn jumping, but I noticed that as the day wore on, Orville was more apt to hit the top instead of clearing it. This was at least a ray of hope; he'd never make it at night.

The barn was now under high construction. I had one room and a bath on the lower level that I could live in. It was getting to look like a home—well, *sort* of like a home. The upper level was still a loft, and this open-sesame top left all doors available to Orville who arrived uninvited at any hour.

One lovely Saturday morning I woke up and sensed something staring at me. Through the slits of my baby blues, I saw Orville peering down at me from the loft. Smack into my youth bed.

"My God, Orville, you frightened the bejesus out of me." I shouted at him, the peevishness very much at home in my voice.

"Hell, lady, it's such a beautiful day, you just going to sleep through it?"

That snapped it. Once again I had the courage to speak to Ella the Eski. "Look," I said, "I'm glad that Orville takes such a wild interest in the house and the building that's going on." (He had dutifully reported every single boner that had been pulled from septic tank to roofing shingles.) I certainly preferred to have Orville as a friend than as an enemy, so I couched my words carefully with lots of smiles. "He's certainly special and graceful . . . But please, Ruth, can't you keep him away from me in the morning? I don't like to get up—I stay up late. I'd appreciate it."

Ruthie gave several admirable grunts and smiled her snaggly smile. "Orville, he never goes to you before eight. I would not let him."

So much for the Lady from the Land of the Midnight Sun.

There was only one more solution to the Orville problem. I had the fence. I could electrify it, but chances were I'd be the one to touch it with wet hair. A gun wouldn't do any good. Orville would merely shoot back.

Peter Carpenter, as usual, came up with the solution.

"Buy yourself a big, ugly, ferocious dog."

"Of course!" I laughed with glee at the thought of a vicious Doberman tearing Orville to shreds while I, the Big Ten, and Ruthie looked on, eating our slices of cold caribou. "I'm afraid of Doberman pinschers."

"Well, then get a dachshund. They bark a lot."

"I know, and I hate dogs that bark."

"Well, get yourself some kind of mutt. At least you'll be forewarned and you can hide in the bathroom until he goes away."

That's why I got Clovis, the trick dog. I bought her at a dog show. Well, not really—I bought the *idea* of her at a dog show held on the Old Gosling High School football field. No dogs are ever for sale at this show. In fact, you insult everyone connected with canine clubs if you try to set a price on Chou Chou of Chowderhead Farm.

"She's not for sale!" Mama Chowderhead shouted at me through the screen of her station wagon. "She's in the show."

"Okay, Okay, I was just shopping. Besides," I said peevishly, "I don't want that breed." I knew that would get to her. "I want . . ." and I pointed around till I saw it, "I want *that* breed."

I didn't have any notion what it was, except that it was the size of a good pony, had a lot of gray hair, and was snoring. "That's what I want."

"Oh, those are Old English," she snarled.

The man who owned the tower of snores assured me that Bartholomew was about to be a daddy in a few weeks (believe me, it didn't show). If I passed the qualifications, I could probably snap up one of his heirs for a few hundred dollars.

"A few *hundred* dollars!" I gasped. Where were the two-dollar dogs Pa used to bring home?

Her name was Clovis from the beginning. I knew she would protect me, chew up Orville, scare his children, do tricks, bring in the newspaper, fetch firewood, sleep at my feet, and never run away. The first day, when she threw up four times, I felt well, what the hell; she's a stranger. Little did I know that she could do much better than that.

The first Sunday she ate about one hundred caladiums, and we met Dr. Mann, Old Gosling's own veterinarian.

"She's got an undershot jaw."

How's that for putting the barb in right away?

"She's sick. What's the matter with her?" I snarled. How would he have liked it if I talked about the wart on his nose?

"Give her these twelve-dollar pills and she'll be just fine. Then bring her in for her shots, and I'll fix her up."

My first problem was to start training Clovis to chase the Commando away. I read *Training You to Train Your Dog* right off. I did pretty well, but Clovis couldn't get the hang of it at all. Okay, old dear, I thought, if stubbornness is your thing, we'll go to school.

Old Gosling just happened to have a training school run by a very muscular lady in bell-bottoms and a beret. The class was held in the school gymnasium right by the Village Green.

Clovis fell the minute she hit the polished gym floor and Miss Blaum, the instructress, immediately took on the hates for her.

"Okay, watchit, watchit, what do you think you're doing?"

I helped Clovis up and we tried to walk on the floor. Down she got on her belly and down she stayed. I hauled her about the floor like a big furry sled.

"Get up, Clovis, for the love of heaven, here comes Blaum."

"Arright class, now either you run your dog or it will run you." As an aside to me (the favorite in the class already), she yelled, "Get that dog up on her feet and in this line. *Noooooooow.*"

I had never been very good in gym, and here I was again the target of some damned gym teacher's frustrations.

"Clovis, please. If you don't come with me, I'll

give you to Muscles Blaum," I mumbled under my breath.

That did it. She rose warily to her feet and followed me meekly to the line. So what if she fell a lot!

"Heel, one two three, heel; sit, stand, walk, heel."

Clovis and I spent every Friday night with Miss Blaum, and the class got smaller and smaller.

I tried to resin Clovis' feet, but it didn't matter. On trial night, Clovis threw up her dinner, but like any good strong mother, I merely cleaned her up and made her go. We flunked. The audience enjoyed her a lot, though, and I still felt that she had "trick" possibilities. After all, all the other dogs had done just the ordinary things like heel, sit, walk, fetch. Clovis —and I don't want you to think that I have any conceit about it—Clovis was the only one that showed any originality. She went to sleep during the retrieve part of the show.

We enrolled again, but this time Miss Blaum was not the teacher. We had a rather nice lady who ran a lot in Davidow slacks, her bosom heaving to and fro in her Maidenform one-piece. Just as I suspected, she immediately sensed that Clovis had talent and came right over after class.

"I must say your dog responds nicely for the first class."

"Yes, doesn't she?" I said smugly, flattered as all hell. Neither Clovis nor I let on it was our seventeenth lesson.

We saw the entire course through until retrieving time. This time Clovis got so carried away with her intelligence that she retrieved the teacher's handbag and made us both suspect. I figured Clovis had learned all she ever had to learn, and we quit just before we didn't graduate.

Clovis is now thoroughly trained. She can watch anything. The only problem—and it's not her fault, it's her breed's—is that she can't see. And when I shout for her, she hears echoes that send her off wildly in the wrong direction. But she does try.

Actually, I had to put a stop to her jumping over the fence with Orville. Even though he didn't hurt his head when he hit the top rail, Clovis was getting quite punchy.

It most certainly wasn't difficult to find a love name for the barn. "Day's End," "Halfway House," "Do Drop Inn," "Shangri-La," weren't quite right. I called it Versailles, not because of its looks, but because of its cost. The contractor, in fact, often mistook me for Louis XIV.

The simple two bedrooms, floor, fill, tuck-pointing, septic tank, well, stone, cement, fireplace, chimney, brick, tile, etc., added up to a considerable bit more than I had had in mind. No matter what I did, it cost $400. I could barely get my paycheck cashed in time to meet the cement truck lumbering up the road. Then there was a series of hands-out people who made up the kingdom's payroll—the road man, the fill man, the lawn man, the gravel man.

When I finally decided on the right color to paint it, I knew that I had hit a winner when the painter refused to put it on.

"Can't be right," he phoned my office.

"I had it specially mixed."

"It's a godawful shade of yukky tanny."

"Great."

"You'll be sorry."

I wasn't.

Well, now, I thought, as the first buds appeared on the trees, *I'll* have some guests. So I had some guests.

Since I had so highly resented my days as coolie labor, I did not ask anyone to help. I became my own coolie labor. I went up early on Friday and scrubbed. By the time I had cooked and cleaned and shopped and toted and washed and mopped and swept, it was Sunday night and time to head back to the city. I had to find some help. I advertised in the swinging Old Gosling *Press*. The only response I had was from the Want Ad lady who wanted to know if she should continue to run the ad.

To save my fingertips and to divert my guests, we all indulged in the local sport of the area, antiquing. Old Gosling was in the heart of antique land. There were at least thirty shops within a radius of three or four miles of the barn. And I always adored having something old to polish and stain and recover.

Most of the barn's furniture came from other peoples' garages or from Mr. Violet's shop. Mr. Violet was my major resource for chairs, irons, and samplers. I got one sampler that was over a hundred years old with Abigail Strawborn and her birthday cross-hatched on it. For years I thought the poor child's name was Strawborn, Abigail Strawborn, until someone pointed out that it was Abigail Straw and she was "born" on Feburary 10, 1881.

Mr. Violet had pink cheeks and ruffly hair and wore plaid pants, bedroom slippers, and mittens. Whenever I found anything I liked, we'd begin this very same conversation:

"Mr. Violet, how much are these cut-glass cruets?"

"Why, I just bought them yesterday at an auction."

"How much do you want for them?"

"Pretty, ain't they? Pity the lady had to sell, but her kids wanted her out of the house. She just set there and wept. When these cruets were sold, she cried out loud. Don't ever trust your kids."

"I won't. How much?"

"Don't know for sure. I'll have to look up the bill. I paid, I think, I paid five dollars for them. I've got to get at least five and a quarter for them."

At this juncture, he rustled out his old order book and pointed to some note of five dollars. "See there, five dollars. Can't let them go for less than five and a quarter. No profit in that, is there?"

Whatever Mr. Violet couldn't sell, Mrs. Violet had bought. "*She* bought it," he'd whisper disdainfully. "*She* bought it, paid too much for it."

So antiquing it was every Saturday. My guests usually managed to refrain from doing anything but looking, or they'd spend a big two bucks while I went wild buying up entire sets of hotel china, plates weighing in at five pounds each and platters at twenty. The more I antiqued, the less money I had and the more I had to clean. I was becoming desperate to get someone to help. I asked everyone, the plumber, the contractor, the bank. No doubt about it, a cleaning lady was Old Gosling's rarest commodity.

One morning I asked the liquor lady.

"Don't you know anyone? I'm bushed. I can't go

on like this. I'll have to sell." Of course, she hated to lose a prize customer like me, so she cased the shop and shut the door. I thought she might pull down the shade.

"Maybe Mrs. Firenza has a day."

Like the Mafia, I had had a tip. The rest was up to me. The Italian ladies of the community—the old ones anyway—were known from one end of the town line to the other as the best cleaning ladies in the county.

"She worked for Mrs. Olson and Mrs. Olson died. Now maybe she's gotta day open. Don't tell nobody. You go see her yourself."

Mrs. Firenza lived in a pretty frame house right in town. I knocked. The door opened slightly to reveal a handsome little woman with white hair pulled back like Maria Ouspenskaya.

"Mrs. Firenza?" I whispered.

"Yah, who wants her?"

"I do. I'd like to talk to her. Are you Mrs. Firenza?"

"Yah, I'm Mrs. Firenza, what you want?"

"I heard that you are a superb cleaner and that you might have a day to spare."

Even though there wasn't a soul on the street, we whispered.

"How you find out dat. Who tol' you?"

"Mrs. Valenzanti, at the liquor store, told me."

"Yah, Mrs. Valenzanti tol' you, huh? She knows everything, huh?"

I peered through the screen, trying to turn on all my pro-Italian charm. "She's a very kind lady, she's helped me a lot. I begged her to tell me."

"She's okay. We're both from Genoa."

"Italy is beautiful." I figured that would cinch it.

"Oh, you like Italy, huh?" She seemed to warm up.

"I love Italy."

"Yah? Well, you can have it. I takka dis country. My sister don' even have water in da house. She has to carry it on her head and go to da river to scrub da clothes. That weighs fifty pounds."

"I only come on weekends," I pleaded, "and I desperately need someone to just get the house open and cleaned up after I leave."

"What kinda house you got?"

I thought it would be a tactical error to break this to her just yet. "I live over on the north side of Great Pond. You know where the Inn is?"

"Of course, I know where da Inn is, you think I'm dumb?"

"Oh, no. I thought you might know the place."

"It's far."

"Oh, it's not that far. You have a car, don't you?"

"Sure I gotta a car, but in da winter, I dunno."

"Oh, please, Mrs. Firenza, try it."

"You not there all week? I gotta work by myself?"

"Well, you could come on Saturday if you'd rather I was there."

She stamped her foot. "I don' work on no Satta-day."

"Well, any day you like."

"Sattaday is my day off. I'm human, too. Okay, I'll look."

She came the next Saturday. "You call dis a house? It'sa barn."

"Well, only the outside. Come in and look."

"You make all dis out of a barn, huh?"

I gave her the dollar tour.

"This pretty good, but my God, lady, it'sa big."

"It's all wood and vinyl and Formica and there's a dishwasher."

"Okay, but it's just a try. I'll give you Thursday night and Monday noon." I didn't care if she came at dawn with Orville. I had help.

Later that week, the switchboard operator at work rang me. "It's somebody from Old Gosling, Connecticut, called Mrs. Firenza. She's calling collect. Should I take it?"

"Yes, yes," I shouted nervously. I just knew she was going to quit. I picked up the receiver gingerly with a sinking feeling. "Hello, Mrs. Firenza, how are you?"

"Hellooa, Missa Tray, you okay?"

"Yes, fine, how are you?"

"Me, I'm fine, pretty good for an old lady."

"That's good."

"Missa Tray, what did you plant out in front there?"

"Oh, Mrs. Firenza, some zinnias and marigolds."

"Yah, I thought so. You like them, huh?"

"Well, I don't have much luck with gardens, but I thought these would be pretty. If they grew."

"Okay, I just checkin' up." She then asked a few more-pertinent questions and hung up. I breathed a sigh of relief.

The zinnias and the marigolds did bloom. In fact, they were the best flowers I had ever touched in my life. Perhaps this was the beginning of a new life I might have with plants. I decided to play Mrs. Miniver and cut some down and put them in my sunbonnet.

Mrs. Firenza, who sometimes included me as one of her day-off entertainments, watched. "You cuttin' the flowers, huh?"

"Yes. Aren't they pretty?"

"Sure dey good flowers, but lissen, Missa Tray, next time you plant don' put dem so close together. It took me all morning to do dem over."

"What are you trying to tell me, that I didn't plant them right? Just look at them, they're beauties."

"Sure, Missa Tray, but I replant every one of dem. Otherwise dey choka."

From that day I guess Mrs. Firenza took an added pleasure in the place. Frequently I'd hear from her by phone about the goings-on in my little chez. Thanks to her and her cheerful earfuls, I got to know about the other life in my house.

"Missa Tray, how are you?"

"Fine, Mrs. Firenza, and you?" I sat eating my eraser waiting for the blow. "And you?"

"Oh, me, I'm pretty good for an old lady. Everything fine here in the house last weekend?"

"It looked fine to me, Mrs. Firenza."

Now it was coming. "You didn't see no snakes?"

There it was. "No. Heavens, no. I didn't see no snakes."

"Wella, Missa Tray, I tella you, I kill da baby snakes," she said proudly. "Three of dem."

Relief. "Oh, I am glad, Mrs. Firenza. Thank you so much. You are brave."

"Well now listen, Missa Tray, you didn't see da mama did you?"

So that was it: a mother snake was loose in my closet.

"I'll tell you, Mrs. Firenza, if I do see the mother snake, you'll be able to locate me at the Inn."

This was funny. She laughed hysterically. "What'sa mattah, Missa Tray, you scared of da snakes? It's nothin' but a litta garter snake."

"I don't care if it's a worm. I'll run. What'll I do, Mrs. Firenza? Whom can I call?"

"Listen, I'll get her if I see her, don' worry, Missa Tray, don' worry."

"Please look for her."

"But now listen, Missa Tray, if you see her, give her a whack with da shovel. That's good, it cutsa dem in half."

I don't know why I wanted to pursue the subject. Lord knows it wasn't going to make me happier or more at ease in Versailles, but like biting on a sore tooth, I had to stay with it.

"Have you seen snakes before, Mrs. Firenza, around the house?"

"Sure, Missa Tray, dis is snake country. You can't live in da country and not see a snake. Hey, what you think?"

"Have you seen them in the house before?"

"Sure, you kiddin', Missa Tray. I see dem all of da time, but I say, why tell her, why worry her . . . Missa Tray, dey won't hurt you, but dis time I missa da mothah. My aim's not so hot anymore, Missa Tray, I'm gettin' to be an old lady . . . but you got good eyes, you keepa dem open."

What the hell, I'd keep them open. With the genius of the dog world guarding the outside and making friends with every viper in sight, and Mrs. Firenza inside missing da mama, I figured the best buy I could make was a large economy size of antitoxin snake venom. Since Clovis showed no inclination to bite Orville's leg, perhaps she'd deign to chew on mine when the viper struck.

V

Despite all the tortures of the carpenters, stone masons, and bricklayers, I prided myself on one asset the property had that wouldn't cost me a nickel. There were hundreds and hundreds of trees. This might not seem so important to anyone who has the knack of growing things, but unlike my family I had not inherited the famous "Hennessy Green Thumb."

Mama had it, Pa had it. Grandma could pick up a branch run over by a Ranger bicycle, put it in a Welch's grape-jelly jar and have a tree a day later. I had inherited, however, like some illegitimate daughter of a Merovingian, the curse of the "black thumb."

I was always sensitive about my thumb. But since my last visit to the plant store—where I touched a plant and I watched five healthy leaves go hurtling to their death—I had become defensive about my killer capacity. I'd have to be careful on walks in my woods not to touch the trees.

The prettiest tree in my kingdom lived right in front of the barn and I had designed the driveway around it. It was a huge triple-trunked elm that turned a startling gold in the fall. Just to the left of that was a black pear, some maples, a few white birches, and then my unlimited woods.

I'd be out of money a lot faster than I'd be out of trees. At least that's what I thought. However, Mrs.

Firenza had other notions. The first weekend in June when I opened the door, a note in her all-too-familiar scrawl fell to the floor, an omen for the weekend.

It read, "What'sa mattah with dat elem? It's losin' all its leaves already?"

This was typical fare. Not to tell me what she thought was wrong or not, but let's torture Missa Tray with a little quizzy.

I called her.

"Hello, Mrs. Firenza, how are you?"

"Ohhhh, Missa Tray, how are you?"

"I'm fine and you?"

"Ohhhhhh, me, I'ma pretty good for an old lady."

There was no use beating around this bush. "Mrs. Firenza, I just read your note about the tree. What do you think?"

"Wella now, Missa Tray, dat tree looks sick to me."

"What's it got?"

"It'sa gotta die."

"Oh, Mrs. Firenza, it's such a pretty tree. What on earth could be wrong with it?"

"I dunno, Missa Tray, but I'ma goin' to send my nephew Tony Paladino over. He's good on trees. He'll tell you right off what it will cost to chop it down."

With a snappish crack in my voice, I snarled, "That tree isn't going to get cut down. I'm going to save that tree. It's an important tree, not just some old twig in the forest. I'll get a tree surgeon."

"Missa Tray, no tree surgeon goin' to save dat elem, it'sa goin' to die for sure."

"Nevertheless, I'm going to check it out. Then if I need Tony, I'll call you." She knew I was mad.

"Wella, you do what you wanna do, it's your money, but dey charge a lota money for lunch for a tree, and you ain't going to save dat elem."

Just for once I was not going to give in to her iron will or her iron family. If worse came to worse, I'd collect its leaves and bark and paste them up again on the first moonlight night.

I phoned Arnie's Arboretum and asked for Arnie. (Why fool around with neighborhood doctors? Go to the top man when you're sick.)

"Arnie," I said, "you come highly recommended. I have a beautiful old elm that's shedding its leaves like crazy, and they only just came out of their buds. I wondered what the matter could be."

"That so." Arnie's was a nice noncommittal answer.

"What do you think it is?"

"Don't know, could be one of two or three things."

"Can you make a . . . a . . . yard visit?" I asked, searching for the right phrase. I think he would have preferred a "house call."

"Don't know if I can make it today."

"Oh, please, Arnie, I might lose this beauty if we wait too long, and I'm only here on weekends." I pleaded with him for a few minutes of his valuable time.

"Well, you know it costs somethin' to come out."

"Oh, that's okay, the elm is important."

Now I'd done it, tipped off the man to my wanton disregard of money to save my tree. The worst possible kind of chess playing. By now, I have learned to ask for a written estimate from the ambulance even if I am on the roadside run over. Why had I refused this day of all days to ignore the laws of financial survival in Old Gosling?

Arnie was the perfect tree surgeon. He arrived in a dusty dump truck. He had a dog, a deep sunburn, an unshaven chin, and the best case of B.O. I'd been near since the girls' gym in high school.

"Oh, Arnie, look. What's the matter with it?"

As we stood there, the leaves kept falling on me and Arnie and Clovis. Arnie's Weimaraner thought Clovis was adorable, but Clovis seemed to have no feelings for Old Socks (that was his name). Clovis was socially maladjusted, I knew, but I didn't feel too bad. Socks, who was supposed to be smart as all "git out," was mounting Clovis' head.

Both Arnie and I tried not to notice and went back to our problem. Let Socks figure it out for himself.

"Well, what do you think?"

"Can't tell till I get up there. It sure looks sick."

"It's such a beautiful tree, tripled trunked and majestic."

"Don't see what you're so concerned about. It's nothing but a piss elm."

I could not believe my ears. "Well, what's it got?"

"Could be Dutch elm blight. There's a lot of it hereabouts. They'll go like the chestnuts one of these years."

"Is it *the* blight?" I moaned, making it sound like the plague in Charles II's time. "The blight, the blight." I would have to run across the fields and into Old Gosling to warn the citizens.

Arnie deftly climbed up the trunk of the tree and examined a leaf, rubbing it between his fingers like a ten-dollar bill. He then hacked at the bark with his penknife. I turned away—I never could stand the sight of sap.

"Don't look like the blight to me."

"Oh, thank God, thank God." My child had been steamrollered and came away unscathed. "What else could it be?"

"You know what?" he said, wiping his face with a shirt tail that had never seen Cold Power, "I think the tree is dying for lack of water."

Then it dawned on me. I was the one who had doomed my priceless elm to hideous death. For ten dollars, old sharp-eye me had gotten the bulldozer man to fill in all the ruts and holes in the lawn and grade it before he took the machinery away. Bravely, I told Arnie the truth.

"Elms are peculiar. They don't like anything on their ankles."

"Is there something we can do? I simply have to save that tree. And Arnie," I added, "there are others that have been filled in."

We walked around and I pointed out the problems.

"Best thing to do is, we'll dig some wells around the trees, starting with the elm. Then you can throw the hose in and let it run. If she wants a drink, she'll live."

"Oh, Arnie, swell. How much will all this cost?"

"Can't tell. Depends on how many, how deep, how long, and how much brick."

"You have to brick them in?"

"Well, if you don't brick them in, first rain and the mud'll be on their ankles again."

I could no more resist his sales talk than I could have chopped down the elm. "Okay, but try to keep it low."

Mrs. Firenza could not believe her eyes the following day when Big Arnie, the Kildare of the elm world, arrived with four husky teen-agers bearing a load of bricks and bags of cement. The Weimaraner got right on Clovis' head, and Mrs. Firenza gave him a swat with her broom. I felt that unless she was curbed, she'd give Arnie one, too.

"What'sa mattah with your dog, Arnie, ain't he got no manners?" Swoop went the broom again. Socks artfully stepped aside and Mrs. Firenza leveled Clovis. What with Orville's high jumps and Mrs. Firenza's blows it was little wonder she was behind in school.

Clovis stumbled into the house away from it all. The crew went to work digging huge holes around the trees. Mrs. Firenza beckoned to me at the door. "Missa Tray, what in da name of God you doin'?" She really was upset with me.

"Oh, Mrs. Firenza, you'll understand when it's finished. Arnie is digging wells so the trees can have a drink."

I had to admit I sounded as loonie as Arnie. She crossed her arms and said quietly, "Missa Tray, dat tree is dead. Dead. Right now. Thissa minute. That elem issa dead."

"How can you be so sure?" I asked her crossly.

"My Tony was here to give the price for cutting it down. He say it'sa dead as a churchmouse. He knows."

I marched right out to Arnie and his crew. He had put his safari hat on to get ready for the big spray. I confronted Arnie and pointed at Mrs. Firenza.

"Arnie, Mrs. Firenza says the tree is dead. Are you sure it isn't?"

He was way up in the elm, tied in his mountain climber's rope. He yanked to be let down. One of the huskies undid the rope and down swooped Arnie, graceful as an eagle.

Mrs. Firenza backed right into the house on the pretense of getting something.

"Coward," I mumbled. She wasn't about to face the wrath of the good surgeon.

"Arnie, Mrs. Firenza's nephew, who is also in trees, says this is a waste of time and money and that the elm has died already."

Arnie was justifiably furious. "Well now, ma'am, if she knows so almighty much about this here elm, let *her* fix it."

"Oh, it isn't that. I'll take your word for it—it's just that she tries to protect me since I don't know an elm from an oak."

"More'n likely she's trying to protect her relative's interest," Arnie retorted sharply. He had a point.

To change the subject and get him back on the job, I admired Arnie's agility with his rope trick.

"That's really nifty," I flattered him, "the way you just grab the rope and head for the sky."

His I'm-just-a-big-boy smile appeared and lit his face. "Shucks, it's nothin'. Anyone can do it. I've been in trees since I was a baby."

I believed that! "Well, it looks like it would be fun," I said, "but I couldn't do it."

Before I could walk a step, Arnie had me laced to him, his right arm around me. My nose, unfortunately, was deep in his armpit.

"No, no, Arnie," I whimpered, "I don't want to . . ."

But Arnie gave the signal to his huskies to pull. We started rising. Before I could scream, we were off the ground twelve feet and heading straight up to God.

The boys shouted with pleasure at the sight of us: Tarzan and Jane in their home away from home. As we sailed by the upstairs windows, Mrs. Firenza loomed into view, caught sight of us, and dropped her mop. Her mouth opened, and she shouted something, but I didn't hear a word. (My screams were most piercing and it would be hard to hear anything above them.) In fact, they were so high I had a fleeting thought that probably every dog in the vicinity would come running.

From way up now I saw Mrs. Firenza with Clovis tagging after her. When Clovis heard me screaming, she turned on her paws and headed in the opposite direction. By God, you could count on that dog!

"Hey, Missa Tray." Mrs. Firenza cupped her message around her mouth. "What you doin' up in dat tree, for da love of God? You gonna breaka your neck."

I couldn't answer. I didn't know what was making me sicker—the height or Arnie's own Arpege. I didn't dare complain for fear he'd drop me. We banged against the bark and Arnie leaned on the big center trunk to rest his hand.

"Grab hold of the branch and just stand there," he commanded. For the first time he saw the reds of my eyes, the vessels popping from the altitude.

"Please take me down," I pleaded.

Arnie laughed, grabbed me again, and up we went higher and higher. I couldn't see Mrs. Firenza, but I could hear Socks and Clovis barking with joy.

"Hey, you fresh thing, you bringa Missa Tray down. She don' like it up there. You hear, you fresha thing!"

Thank God for Mrs. Firenza!

I could see them coming, I could see them running: the Hendersons. They wouldn't miss out on this scene, nosiree. First Orville leaping over the fence, then Ruthie and the Big Ten. It dawned on me at that very moment, like a God-given revelation, that Ruthie wasn't pregnant. She'd been like that since I met her, and that was a hell of a lot longer than it takes to make a Henderson (although they were tougher, so maybe they did take longer). It's funny what thoughts you have before dying.

Mrs. Firenza, who knew how little I enjoyed their visits, tried to play it cool by saying at the top of her lungs, "It'sa nothin,' Orville, nothin.' Missa Tray is up da tree, dat's all."

How right she was: we had reached the summit. Nothing left now to do but plant the United States flag and head home.

"Please, Arnie, let's go down. I'm getting sick."

All the Hendersons thought it was great fun. They had no idea I liked to play like this. Why, who knows? I might turn out to be human after all! To join in on the frolic, Orville hopped on to the bottom branch, and I merely prayed that he wouldn't rock the tree too much. If it kept up, the whole damned tree might come down a lot faster than even Tony Paladino thought.

Mrs. Firenza got the boys to lower the boom by hitting them with her broom. Then, like a descent from heaven, we appeared right smack in the middle of the crowd.

"What you try to do, killa Missa Tray? What kinda man does things like dat? Huh, you answer me."

I was too bushed to say anything. I just leaned on the tree and thought seriously of kissing the earth.

"Dead trees are verra dangerous," Mrs. Firenza said spitefully.

Arnie undid the rope and looked her right in the eye. "That tree ain't dead yet."

"Dat tree hassa been dead for a month," she spit back at him.

The fight was on. The Hendersons agreed with Mrs. Firenza. In fact, Orville 'lowed how it was dead as a wooden door, which I liked better than Mrs. Firenza's churchmouse metaphor.

Arnie said he'd save that tree if it cost him his life. Instead, it cost me $345 plus bricks. The ride I got was free.

The next Monday my call from Old Gosling came in right on time.

"Missa Tray, how you?"

"Oh, I'm fine, Mrs. Firenza, and you?"

"Ohhh a, I'ma pretty good for an old lady."

"How's everything?"

"Wella, Missa Tray, almost everything is fine. It'sa dose holes datta man dug dat are causing all da trouble."

"Why, what happened?"

"Da garbage man slipped in da big hole by da elem. He didn't see da hole. He *and* da can went in."

"Oh, God, was he hurt?"

"No, he wasn't nothin' but shook up. But Missa Tray, you better take care of dose holes or someone is gonna fall and hurt themselves. Yes."

"Yes, I'll do it right away."

"Okay, Missa Tray. Meanwhile I'll pray to God dat no one goes in."

By Friday the elm had lost considerable ground. In fact, there were more leaves in the well than there were on the tree. I dug them out, ran the hose, and had the hardware man put on screens. It wasn't bad. Twenty-five dollars covered all the holes. (Arnie didn't do that kind of work.)

The next weekend the tree was bare. I called Arnie.

"Arnie, the elm is bare."

"Guess we didn't catch her in time."

"Guess we didn't. Could you take one last look."

I figured the least thing that bastard could do was hold a mirror in front of it and sign the death certificate.

Dump truck, B.O., and Socks arrived. "Yep, she's gone." He peered into the wells. "See you had them covered. That was smart."

"What about all the others? Are they going to die, too?"

"Can't tell yet. They look okay."

"What will I do with this one?" I patted the piss elm's hand. "I guess it could get by the winter."

"You better cut that down. She'll take your roof off if she falls in a storm."

"How much will that cost?"

"Don't know. That's not our work." He started the motor of the dump truck. "We only *save* trees."

As he went through the gate, he shouted, "When fall comes, I'll plant you a real pretty tree where the piss elm was."

Mrs. Firenza was polishing the pewter, a chore she rarely cottoned to.

"Dissa pewter, it'sa lotta work, Missa Tray, but it'sa pretty."

She was being sweet because she knew that I was ready to sell the house, the pewter, the piss elm, and her.

"Boy, wasn't Arnie a gem?"

"He'sa no good. You getta my nephew Tony and he will cut down da tree and he willa save da others."

"Tell him to cut them all down. I'll get Japanese parasols," I said bitterly.

"Hey, you verra funny, Missa Tray. You gonna get a nice cord, maybe two, three cord of wood from dat elem."

I was livid. Every dime I earned was going down the drain in Old Gosling. These little extras were killing the golden goose. Well, what the hell, I could always burn the place down and collect insurance—God knows I had enough wood for a real beauty. But then there was the consoling thought that three thousand lousy years from now, when some adventurous archeologist digs up my front lawn, he will be bound to think some ravishing Inca princess had herself bricked in after the bloodletting ceremonies.

VI

Some people store up their money in paintings, others choose the Wall Street route. I console myself with the fact that when I'm old and gray, I can always peddle the antiques I am buying today. The second I get my hands on my first old-age check I'll put on my Shaker bonnet and put out a sign, "Aunt Jane." Or better yet, "Missa Tray's Olde Antique Shoppe." Then I can cash in on my footbaths, mariner's horns, and butterfly plates. They should all be older and more valuable, which is more than I can say for anything I bought from the New York Stock Exchange. They might even be genuine antiques by then.

Certainly, I've had enough antique experience to run a good show. I've been to so many shops up and down Old Gosling Road that I can tell at a glimpse of the shutters what period they excel in, what kind of markup, what kind of merchandise they'll house, and what form of creature runs the place.

If the house is painted a *House Beautiful* color, the steps brick, the plants potted, and there's a trickling fountain of a little elf peeing on the terrace, you know you have faggots. However, if you see something you want and are willing to wait till the boys are bored and want to hit the Acapulco sun in season, chances are you'll get a buy. That's how I got my brass birdcage for ten dollars.

If the house is just an old shack with an oil burner, drippy-nosed kids, a mongrel dog, and a corn patch with some zinnias, you might well find a treasure. That's where I got my tole footbath for two dollars. On the other hand, you might well buy some Sandwich glass which came from the famous Woolworth Estate, the five-and-dime.

But if the house is truly restored and only the owner's name is on the sign without the added come-on "Antiques," and there's a line that reads, "By Appointment Only," you know you're into real money. Florence Payne's shop was just such a place. Somehow I had managed to drive by this place, even though there were days when I practically pulled the floorboards up out of the front of the car trying to get loose from my seat belt to get out. I knew there was nothing but trouble ahead in a shop like this, since I'd want everything in it, including Mr. Payne.

Well, the Mintons, some wealthy neighbors (actually their one-hundred-acre estate edged the Old Gosling Inn where we'd met), were coming to see Versailles. Since it was on their way, they had made an appointment with Mrs. Payne. It was my golden opportunity to case the place without putting up a penny. I was with the royal family.

Morris Minton rang the bell, and we could hear the eighteenth-century gong reverberate through the house. Florence Payne graciously opened the door, and in a hushed, reverential tone, Minton told her who he was. Acting like Katharine Hepburn, she told us in a hushed, breathy voice, to "Come in."

Martha Washington showing off Mt. Vernon to the vermin couldn't have been stuffier. However, she warmed up to pure New England after Minton picked out several Battersea boxes he liked. I immediately left them and started poking around the other rooms, trying to see everything this famous collector had collected. This obviously provoked Mrs. Payne because I'm sure she thought I'd steal. Then I saw what I'd been looking for for months. A fireback! A fireback with a beautiful sunburst design on it, a fireback that was huge and would fit my oversize fireplace. I needed a fireback desperately, since the bricks were falling out from the heat. When I complained to the man who put in the fireplace, he gave me a great Yankee answer.

"It's the heat, lady," as if I thought my fires were throwing off crushed ice. "Get a fireback and it'll be fine."

Well, I think everyone should shop for an oversize fireback.

Mrs. Payne, sensing my interest, said, "It's a lovely example, isn't it?"

"Example," that famous antique word, means money.

"It's pure."

Now I knew I was in trouble.

"I picked it up in France." I would have liked to see that, since it must have weighed a half a ton.

I asked the question.

"Eleven," she answered blithely.

I thought for a second—no, a split second—that

she meant eleven dollars, but I squelched that thought in a hurry. Mrs. Payne's pomander balls cost more than that.

"Eleven hundred is high for that, isn't it?" Morris Minton asked.

Mrs. Payne looked hurt. "My dear man, it's a steal. I got it from a chateau. Undoubtedly it's Louis'; see the sun?"

"Well, so much for firebacks," I said. "Anyway, I can't light a fire till the starlings clear out."

For a month I had been sharing my house and hearth—especially the hearth—with a family of starlings. Though most communities hire a man with a pan to chase starlings away, I just didn't have the heart to burn the babies. However, they weren't as generous with me. They chirped at dawn. What started out as a peep up at the top of the chimney stack, ended up a blast down where I lived. This, plus the bonuses all birds leave and their lice, made me less inclined to like birds than ever. I had never even cut the pages of a book someone gave me when I was eight, called *The Birds of America,* since I had requested a medical kit. Nevertheless I had to admit the starlings were the only birds I ever saw in Old Gosling. Evidently the word hadn't gotten out that the food at Missa Tray's was extraordinary.

People who visited me always saw birds through bird glasses. When I observed the scene, I saw nothing but a dead tree or a new wasp nest.

"Oh, look! A golden-winged pancake! they'd shout, but when I got there it was nothing but a sparrow.

Purple grosbeaks and bald eagles were always popping up in the Old Gosling *Press,* but I had yet to lay eyes on the bird of Old Gosling itself, the oriole.

"Leave out string, and orioles will build their nests with it." I left out enough string for them to weave a rug, but they never so much as picked it up. Birds aren't very grateful. Meanwhile, down at my closest neighbors, the Hendersons, I saw cardinals, jays, and blackbirds. Every kind of bird was always swooping down on their lawn. One guestless Saturday afternoon I decided to find out just what enticing Eskimo delicacy Ruthie was flinging out to them.

I had never been in the Henderson house before. If I had had any sneaking fancies that they were pigs, I scored it firmly the moment I stepped in. They were real Swamp Yankees—that's the sharecropper of New England. Ruthie was chopping up some raw elk, and they cleared off a chair for me to sit on. This was indeed a twist—for me to be in their house. And that house was pure amazement. I had always thought Eskimos kept up a fairly neat igloo, but this integrated Nanook had forsaken all hope of ever cleaning up this ice floe. She had turned over the entire running of the household to their seventeen-month-old baby, who was scrambling whale blubber in a large skillet.

All the major equipment and an old sofa were outside on the front porch. In the living room stood a rusty old boat, upside down on two rusty barrels. All the chairs in the place had springs sprung from long years of sitting. They curled around and out of the cushions like vipers. The world's largest television set was screaming away, and as Ruthie chopped, she watched Julia Child making a *quiche aux fruits de mer*.

"You always have such pretty birds here, Ruthie," I chirped.

She looked at me like I had just left my cage. "Yeh, there's lots of birds around here."

"Do you give them something special to eat that attracts them all?"

The thought of Ruthie feeding birds didn't seem to make any sense to Ruthie. She fed *on* birds. Ruthie shrugged indifferently. "No, I don't give them nothing. Maybe the kids leave their jelly bread outside. Can't think of nothing else." Ruthie made it obvious that she most certainly had no intention of feeding any birds. In fact, she would very likely have fought an oriole to a piece of bread if she thought her nest needed it.

"Well, it's certainly strange how they live down here and never come near my place." I sounded jealous.

Orville thought maybe he knew where some sunflower seeds were. "Maybe the kids gave them those."

Ruthie didn't seem to care one way or the other and resumed getting her elk ready.

Orville looked in vain for the sunflower seeds. He rumbled through a cupboard and into a closet. He unearthed three old quilts and then pulled out a huge old piece of iron. My antique-trained eyes blinked three times.

"Orville, what a beautiful fireback! That's exactly what I've been searching for!"

Orville looked pleased and pointed at the boat. "The boat?"

"No. That!" Orville searched around the closet, pointed at the blankets, then back to the boat. He could not believe that anyone would want this old piece of iron.

"That." I pointed at the fireback.

"That? That's nothin'."

"That's a beautiful fireback."

"Was here when we come. Too heavy for a table. Besides, you couldn't write on it with all the lumps."

"It's a real beauty."

"You want it?"

"Oh, Orville, I'd love it, but I couldn't take it. I'll buy it from you."

I knew a gift from Orville would mean many, many commando tales from the land of the Eskimos.

"I'll buy it from you for ten dollars."

Orville was speechless. He motioned me not to say anything to Ruthie. Ten bucks was going to be his treasure.

When we tried to lift it, we couldn't budge it. Orville decided that we'd put it on a blanket and then lift up the four corners of it. In getting a blanket out of the closet, I noticed behind the pile was quite a collection of Christian Brothers and Manischewitz half pints, some sampled, some almost completely empty. Orville gave me the high-sign again and covered up the bottles with a blanket. And all this time I thought the workmen had left their luncheon wines! For a year I had been finding old sherry bottles and claret bottles and apricot-brandy bottles stashed behind the fence or tucked neatly in the woodpile. It was easy to see Orville's tippling pattern. If Ruthie found one supply, Orville had others carefully staked out. No wonder he wanted that ten dollars kept secret.

Orville helped me lug the fireback home. I gave him his ten bucks, and I had him for another hour. But a pure example of a fireback like this for only ten bucks made Orville's Battle of Guam almost bearable. And I most certainly could tell the Mintons that I had found a fireback in one of Old Gosling's oldest estates—and for only ten!

VII

My own guests were seldom the problem. It was the unknown quantity that occasionally came along with them. Kit and Bob were delights. We seldom got to see each other in the city except for a dinner now and then, and Lord knows they had taken me out in their vintage Volks all too often not to have them at least once in the summer.

Kit called about time and place and then casually added this line:

"Did you ever meet Sandy, Bob's cousin?"

"No, I don't think so." I knew so.

"Well, she's rather offbeat for my taste, but Bob has her on his hands this weekend. We wondered if you'd mind if she came with us. She's kind of a 'loner,' and Bob worries about her. Personally, I think she has a crush on him, but I thought if you didn't mind, we'd haul her along."

Well, what do you say? You say, "Love to have her." Right?

"What does she do?" I thought I'd try to learn a little about her. There was a chance I could invite some other soul to whom I owed a weekend and marry them off.

"She's a photographer. Sort of a Village Bachrach. She's quite bright, but intense, if you know what I mean."

Kit made her sound young and cuckoo. How bad could Sandy be? Maybe I'd get her to photograph Clovis.

"Bring her along, I have enough weeds for everyone."

Kit and Bob arrived as planned on Friday night, but sans Sandy.

"She said she'd be a few minutes late for dinner and not to wait."

Sandy's idea of being late for dinner and mine were quite different. At midnight, Kit and Bob gave up and turned in. At 12:30, when I was having my Perrier and watching *The Return of Zorro,* I heard something that sounded like a motorboat racing up the driveway. I hoped it could stop before it came in. I turned on the driveway lights. "Sandy?" I called hesitantly.

"Sorry, baby. I'm late, but I got all involved."

Her Karmann Ghia was still rocking from the slammed brake stop. Sandy got out and stretched. She wasn't young; she was a leftover from Taos. She had sandy red hair cut short, huge hands, huge feet. She wore a peasant skirt, woven sarape, and Indian sandals. She also had on seventeen rings.

"Lots of fog coming up."

"Yes, it gets that way at night."

"Took me an hour to get up here." (Without the fog, it took me an hour and half.)

I had never met an honest-to-God *old* Bohemian photographer, so I made my first mistake. "Have you eaten?"

"No, and I'm famished."

"Well, I don't know what's left" (I knew damned good and well what was left), "but I'm sure I can dredge up something."

"Actually, baby, I wouldn't mind a drink first, I'm exhausted. Got all involved and simply lost track of time. If I don't set the alarm in the darkroom, I could be gone for days."

She started to unpack the car. I could not believe the amount of luggage. She had two suitcases, twenty-seven cameras, tripods, flashbulbs. Could Kit have invited her for the summer?

"I know it looks like a lot but I hate being away from my equipment."

I wasn't sure she and the paraphernalia would all crush into the guest room. She looked around the place.

"Certainly lost the spirit of the original barn when they fixed this one." (Obviously no one had told her I had fixed it.) "That's the trouble with decorators. Me, I like white walls and cushions on the floor and one decent piece of sculpture. How can people live with all this ancient junk around?"

"We try! Me, I like to sit on a chair now and then," I added caustically. "What do you want to drink?"

"I'd love a frozen daiquiri."

"I don't even know what's in one, let alone how to make it."

She looked at me disdainfully. "Ice, baby, limes, baby, rum, sugar, and a Waring blender."

I got out the ingredients and Sandy took over. Since I had no ice crusher, she cracked the ice in a dish towel by slamming it against the stone wall, discus-thrower style. If this was the cocktail hour, I shuddered for the thought of dinner.

"Got any cheese? I love cheese. It's for-real food."

Well, that was in order. Maybe a slab of cheddar and a daiquiri and we could take the flag down and go to bed.

We sat in the living room while I tried to catch Zorro's last words.

"Turn that garbage off!"

"Oh, I enjoy old flicks. They're funny."

"Then have the decency to collect old Chaplin."

"You're right. Next time I have several grand I'll snap up a few."

"Did you read all the books here or are they wall coverings?"

I'd show her. "Actually, they're printed on the wall. It's a *trompe l'oeil*."

"Hate them, they're so goddamned pretentious."

She walloped out two more daiquiries while I suppressed several hundred yawns. It was now two o'clock—A.M., remember.

"Well, if you're going to eat, I'd better do something about it. I'm falling asleep."

"Nonsense, people sleep too much. Gandhi only needed four hours."

"Good for him. The older I get, the more I need. In fact, at the rate I'm going I'll only be up for an hour on Thursday."

"Better ask your shrink what you're escaping from."

"Offbeat" was hardly the word for Cousin Sandy. Repulsive, I thought, fit her to a T. Being straight out of F. Scott Fitzgerald and old Greenwich Village, she most certainly didn't have the soft love of a flower child.

"Well, what's on the menu?"

"We had a quiche and salad."

"I think I'll just scramble some eggs and bacon."

And so, at three in the morning, Sandy ate our breakfast right down to the blueberries I had cleaned earlier. Then she marched off to bed.

Exhausted, I fell atop my sack and was actually asleep before my head hit the pillow. The next thing I heard was water running. No, it wasn't running, it was thundering; it sounded like someone had found the source of the Nile. Subconsciously, when I don't want to face anything, I pretend that whatever I hear is part of my dream. But this was no dream, it was trouble. I opened an eye and listened. It was just beginning to be light. I looked at my watch—it was a big six thirty. The water in the guest bathroom was gushing forth at the rate of five gallons per second. I didn't think there was that much pressure in the whole house.

I knocked on the bathroom door. Over the sound of the Falls I heard Sandy shout. "Yes, yes, what is it?"

"Are you all right?" I asked cowardly. I wanted to

shout, "Shut off the damned water, you dumb broad."

"Yes, fine, be out in a moment."

From that point on it sounded like a pair of baby seals had been let loose. The odor of my Mémoire Chérie Bath Oil pervaded the entire house and yard. Obviously Sandy had no notion how much Elizabeth Arden recommended.

The water managed to run in the kitchen while I tried to make some coffee. Would wonders never cease. She had left enough water for a pot.

"Well, you are an early bird, after all," she chirped at me pleasantly.

My killer instinct was aroused.

"The hell I am! I thought someone must be sick to get up this early!"

This barb didn't hit her at all. She reached for the pot and asked if *I* wanted some coffee.

"I just want a little something before I get going." She was going away, how wonderful! "I want to go up to Litchfield and take some pictures. I might do you tomorrow."

"I don't want my picture made."

"Nonsense, everyone wants their picture taken." She grabbed my chin and turned my head sidewise to study it. "Otherwise, why mirrors? I'd like to do you in profile."

Standing in my own kitchen at 6:45 A.M. on a Saturday with this counterfeit Steichen holding my head sidewise to see my profile, I growled, "That figures. It's not my best point."

"Silly, it's the only interesting thing about your face."

That snapped it. If my profile—for which I had always wanted to save enough for surgery—was the best of me, God help the people who came in daily contact with me full-face.

"I suppose you're prudish about your clothes."

"How do you mean that?"

"Well, the ideal thing—the study, that is—would be to do a top photo, say from the waist up, no clothes."

"Yes, I'm prudish about clothes."

"Well, see I called the shot on that one! It's a shame 'cause there's a nice slump to your back."

I now watched Sandy eat everything that I had planned for lunch: cold cuts, cheese, crackers, and fruit. "That should hold me until I find a diner."

Hold her? It should have anchored her to the ground.

"Well, I'm just wasting time," she said, pushing back her chair. "Leave my dishes. I'll do them when I get home."

She shouted at me to give her a hand with her equipment, then climbed into her Ghia and raced the motor for a good ten minutes, mixing Mémoire Chérie with high octane. I looked at my watch. It was now 7:20. I would be first in line at the grocery, since the larder was bare. Certainly my adrenalin was too far up now to think of going back to bed.

At noon, Kit appeared fresh and pretty.

"Did Sandy ever show?"

"She showed and has gone to photograph leaves in Litchfield."

Was it possible that she slept through the arrival, the flood, and the departure?

"You didn't hear her?"

"No, I sleep like a log. So does Bob." My mental picture of their hibernation, two huge logs under one of Mr. Violet's patchwork quilts, made me forgive them.

It was a pleasant day. Bob read, Kit did her needlepoint, I weeded. And then Sandy was with us again, making our cocktail hour truly memorable. I had bought a lot of eggs and a lot of food in her honor. I was right on target: she deviled herself six eggs before dinner. Conversation with Sandy was difficult since (1) she didn't dig me, and

    (2) she detested Kit, and

    (3) she liked Bob and didn't want Kit to know it, and

    (4) she had only read *The New York Times* up to 1961.

It had been years since the Profumo trial and she had just caught up on it. So we all talked about Christine, Dr. Tim Leary, and a diet she thought I should go on, consisting of all rice. Pointing to my eyeballs she said, "You're Sanpaku, baby, Sannnpak-kuuuu."

She spent Sunday on my terrace with all her equipment, but when she took a picture, it was always with the same camera. At one point she sat for two hours with her hands inside a black bag.

"What on earth are you doing? Changing rings?"

"Winding film. It's cheaper this way. They just rob you if you buy it all wound."

At Sunday lunch, I doled out the Caesar salad because Sandy attacked the chicken like it was her very first meal after forty days of fasting. She cut off a few slices for Kit and Bob and me and then settled into the bird like an early Tudor king.

Polishing off what was left of the salad, she whipped into the fruit bowl. Bob, teasing her, said, "What's the matter, Sandy, not hungry?"

And deadly serious herself, she said, "You know, I am not. I don't know what's the matter with me today, I must just be off my feed."

"Better see your shrink and find out what's escaping from you," I chided her.

"You're a riot, that's what."

She then took pictures of Clovis with a zoom lens that only the president of Clairol could cherish. By Sunday night everyone was anxious to cut—me mostly. While Kit and I did the dishes, Bob helped Brenda Starr pack up. She shouted down to me. "Got to run now, baby. If ever you want your profile shot, holler."

I seriously considered sending her a bill for hotel privileges. As a matter of fact, I thought that I might apply to Diners' and American Express and ask to be registered as a first-class Inn.

VIII

To my absolute surprise, the barn was more delightful in the winter than in the summer. What had started out as a summer-weekend place was fast becoming my full-time home away from home. I had the heat put in. The furnace chugged and puffed, and the piss elm sparked cozily against my ten-dollar fireback. If the snowplow man didn't show, it was impossible and impassable for anyone to come near the place. Only Ruthie could snowshoe over, and it was so cold that even she had to wear a sweater. (Ordinarily, she could manage in housedresses until December.)

My weekends were the ultimate in peace and quiet. Clovis dreamed in front of the fireplace, and I had time to think. The snow blew and drifted five to six feet deep, covering bushes and stones with dollops of designs. The windows were hung with icy stalactites, the panes covered with kaleidoscopes of frosted patterns. An occasional blue jay—lost, no doubt, from his rightful property—sat for a brief moment on my ugly angel statue to get his bearings. The great added bonus, of course, was there was no weeding, no half-dead flowers—and *all* the trees looked dead, not just mine.

The pond was a sheet of ice. Brooks that had been bog in the summer ran and trickled over pine boughs which had dropped softly at night from the trees. It was so clear and cold and silent all you could hear was the wind pushing and whistling as it shoved and hustled its way down from Canada.

For all of its problems, my barn was as snug as a well-built whaler's ship. It might creak and crack but you knew it was going to stand up under any New England storm. At sunset after a snow, the trees turned black, the sky purple, and I felt like I'd been trapped in a corny phone-company advertisement.

Unlike summer, when people loved visiting and playing in the country, I had full run of my own house. Nobody was that crazy to play in the cold. Obviously I'd spend Christmas in the country, and for that occasion, obviously, I'd invite Peter.

About two days before the holiday, my alert came from Mrs. Firenza.

"Hello, Mrs. Firenza, how are you?"

"Me, I'm fine for an old lady, how you?"

"Me, I'm fine."

"Missa Tray . . ."

"Yes?" I chewed my pencil. Was it a fire, the furnace, the hot-water heater, the snowplow?

"How'sa weather there?"

"We're having a blizzard."

"Yah, we are, too. Some storm, huh, Missa Tray?"

What was behind her weather report? A caved-in roof?

"You know da blue room, Missa Tray?"

"Yes, what's the matter with the blue room?"

"You know what happened, Missa Tray?"

"No. What happened?"

"A partrich flew righta in da blue room."

"A what?"

"A partrich. You know, dem big brown birds."

"You mean there's a live partridge in the blue room?" This *was* a new one.

"No, Missa Tray, it'sa dead, but it flew right in. Guess it got lost in da snow."

"Did it come through a window."

Giggling loudly, she answered, "Hey, Missa Tray, you think it come through da door?"

"So what happened?"

"Such a mess. My God, such a mess. Right through da storm window and da screen and da other window."

"Dead on arrival, yes?"

"Missa Tray, dat bird is a mess."

"Well, that's what he gets for breaking and entering. What about the window?"

"Wella, Missa Tray, I clean it up and I put cardboard in da window, but dat'sa not enough, it's going to be cold tonight, and if da pipes in here get froze, zoomie go da furnace."

"Well, can you call the hardware man?"

"I called Mr. Montani and he says all da trucks are stuck."

"Okay, let me try, and I'll call you back."

Mr. Montani, Old Gosling's most prosperous hardware merchant, was a fair-weather friend. He was not about to go and fix my window in the storm. It was easy to deal with him. I just reminded him of the several hundred minor purchases I had made from him on nice days—like washers and driers and dishwashers and vacuum cleaners and nails and saws and hammers and rakes. He assured me that it would be a pleasure for him personally to get stuck in the snow for me.

By the time I arrived for Christmas, Mr. Montani had fixed the window, and the house was snug and gala. No bloody partridge on my pear tree but lots of gifts from people determined to show their acceptance of my barn life. Like my sister who broods over creative presents for me. If I'd told her once, I told her a hundred times to buy me handkerchiefs, but she wasn't about to give up. Obviously she'd worried about my newfound life in the country until she came up with a winner—a single-artichoke steamer pot—a rundown on my social life by my sister.

From brooding creative friends I got a deviled-egg plate for forty-nine people, or forty-nine half eggs. I got some blue crystals from Neiman-Marcus that I thought were bath crystals. They were sugar crystals. (I made a note to save them for Sandy.) I got a large mesh hat with velvet streamers that you put over huge buffets in Savannah. The real prize, I could hardly wait to give Mrs. Firenza, was a mouse catcher that ejected mice outdoors alive and well, so they could come right back in.

But the present of presents was a simple card from Green Flower Farm. It showed a charming farm under ninety feet of Green Flower snow, a wisp of New England applewood smoking out of the chimney and a little remembrance inside that could have been written by Mary Baker Eddy.

"Merry Christmas and Happy New Year
from
Green Flower Farm and Kit and Bob

Three cork willows and three copper beeches have been specially tagged for you, and when the snow is gone and spring is on the wing, we will send them to you."

A vast improvement on the single-artichoke pot, I'll say that. Kit and Bob knew that I, of all people, was a sucker for trees.

Well, while I waited for my trees, I could try to get some birds used to the idea of sitting in them. There certainly had to be some way to attract them. I spoke to Carl, the butcher, who assured me that a suet ball was the way to attract the colorful birds.

"Suet balls?"

"Yep, they have a love for suet."

He wrapped up a dozen at three for a dollar. I wouldn't eat, but my darlings would. The big greasy things were coated with sunflower seeds, and as I dropped them in strategic places, I felt like St. Elizabeth of Hungary.

The following weekend, I fully expected to fight my way through Alfred Hitchcock's thriller. I didn't see one claw mark. The suet balls were untouched.

Maybe the birds needed a house to eat in. I bought a sack of half-and-half and a split-level birdhouse made of redwood and wrought iron. Cost: $22.95.

Now, my lovelies, I was truly ready for the winged ones. I filled the seed part of the birdhouse and shut the sliding glass door that slipped into place as the seed was eaten. This was to insure the birds, instead of a mouse or a chipmunk, getting the chow.

Then I nailed the house to an old sycamore.

It was working! I noticed action that very after-noon and grabbed the glasses. There was my first tenant. He was all they say about them. Bright-eyed, bushy-tailed. A yellow and black chipmunk. He adored the ranch house and hung upside-down from its ferret-proof door. To and fro he went. Only oc-casionally did he open the glass partition with his back foot so that the seed would pour out, Morton-salt style, right into his hungry black mouth.

I peered at him in utter awe through my bird-watching glasses. He did not like the seed part and spit that on the ground. The birds could have that. He did like the rest and carefully edited it out with his teeth. He never left the house, and if a bird really wanted in, he wouldn't dare try to get near it with "hisself" swinging there. After he had his fill, he curled up on top of the house and slept.

I resorted to Pepperidge Farm bread as my next step to attract fowl. Clovis stepped in here. Bread that she wouldn't touch in the house suddenly took on charm—so much so that she would truffle-hunt for it in the snow like a big fat snorkling pig.

After chasing anything that came in sight that might take her bread, Clovis, exhausted, slipped on the ice and fell down. I knew I should have bought her galoshes. She seemed so stiff I thought she had caught a cold and whisked her off to Dr. Mann. Obviously she had frozen her toes.

I worried over her in his office while he prodded her feet. After he removed several pounds of rock salt and bread crumbs from her toes and pads she perked up considerably. Amputation was not necessary.

When I got home and put Clovis to bed with a hot drink, I marched out and dragged the house away from the chipmunk. It wasn't easy. He held on to the door. I took it to the hardware store and said, "I thought this thing was ferret-proof."

Mr. Montani assured me that this was once again a first.

"You mean you really get chipmunks?"

"I get *one* that sleeps on the roof and opens the gate with his little toe." The truth is, I sounded proud.

"Must be a damned-smart chipmunk."

"You bet."

"Well, I'll tell you what I'd do. I'd not nail it to the tree and I'd hang it with a chain [$3]. No chipmunk will go near a chain."

There wasn't any point in going back to Mr. Montani again. The creature loved the chain so much he would approach it by jumping over two trees and into the feeder. It was actually more fun with the chain. In fact, he got married soon after and lived there with his spouse through the winter.

Then Mrs. Firenza called to remind me that spring was just around the corner.

"Hey, Missa Tray, how you?"

"Fine, Mrs. Firenza, and you?"

"Good," she laughed. "Pretty good for an old lady. Missa Tray, you comin' up this week?"

"Well, I wasn't sure, why?"

"Wella, I tell you. You got a notice about your trees, they here."

"What trees?"

"You got trees by mail. It says dey are now at da post office. Copper beech."

Finally, I remembered. "Oh, yes, someone gave me some trees for Christmas."

She let this pass in her own way, chalking up one more time that I had loons for friends. Who ever gave anyone a tree except God to Joyce Kilmer?

"You gonna try and plant now?"

"Well, it is early, but I guess we could put them in."

There it was again, the voice of doom coming at me.

"It snowed once here in May, Missa Tray."

"Okay, Mrs. Firenza, I'll try and find out."

I phoned Green Flower Farm. Yes, yes, indeed my copper beeches had been balled, tied, and shipped just as they had been instructed to do. They left there on April first and this was the third. They most certainly should have arrived in Old Gosling yesterday.

"I'm not up there on weekdays in the winter, so where are they?"

He reckoned the most likely spot for them would be the railway express office. "Don't leave them in a hot place too long without giving them some water."

I phoned Railway Express. Was there a depot in Old Gosling?

"No, ma'am," the clerk said. "We used to have one but it wasn't worth keeping. You have to go to New Town."

I called New Town. No answer. I called again. No answer. Finally just before five, I caught them.

"I have a package there and I can't pick it up till Saturday."

"Don't make no deliveries on Saturday."

"Well, I'll come get it."

"Ain't open on Saturday."

He went off to check my package.

"Yep, got some trees here."

"When can you deliver them?"

"We already tried three times, lady. Now you'll have to come get them yourself."

"Listen, would you mind throwing some water on their balls?" I asked, trying not to sound too obscene.

"Sure, lady, if it will make you happy. But I think you had better try and pick these up. Soon. Don't look too healthy to me."

I drove up on Friday morning. It was a misty, cold-as-hell gray day. The last of the snow was being rained away, but it looked like there might well be more snow from Vladivostok looming out of the East.

I played the heater full blast and Clovis clung to it.

The man at the Express office was 109 years old that very day and arthritic. He could barely lift the notice, let alone help me with the balled bundles. I dragged and lifted them. Finally, by leaving both back windows open, I managed to get the three of them in. This did not please Clovis, who moved to the front seat and hid with embarrassment as we headed down the highway.

Now that I had the damned things, what could I do with them? After Arnie's elm tragedy you wouldn't think that I'd be on the phone to him, but that's exactly where I could be found. Arnie would have to come into my life again. It wasn't easy to coax him out.

It was pouring rain now. Between the two of us, we managed to get them in the frozen ground.

"I know, don't tell me."

"Tell you what?"

"Don't tell me you don't know whether they'll make it or not."

"Okay, I won't."

Arnie and I drank quite a bit of vodka to warm up, and Clovis wore her sweater to bed. Arnie was vastly more palatable in the winter, when his armpits frosted over.

I had hardly gotten to work on Monday when the phone rang again.

"Missa Tray? How you?"

"I have a bad cold but other than that I'm fine, how are you?"

"Oooohhhh me, I'm pretty good for an old lady.

Hey, Missa Tray, I see you got those trees planted, huh?"

"Yep, frozen ground or no frozen ground!"

"You think they'll live?"

"Sure, they'll live." I was learning to roll with the major jabs.

"Hey, that's good, Missa Tray, I'm glad."

"So what's up?"

"Wella, Missa Tray, you know what come in da mail this morning?"

"No. What?"

"Another one of dem notices you get."

"What kind of notice?"

"Da same kind as last week. Only thissa time you got three corka willow at da station."

IX

I had made up my mind that weeds or no weeds I was giving a major bash on the long Fourth of July weekend. My clients only had a verbal idea of Versailles, and none of Old Gosling's society had been inside. Now was the time for Missa Tray to mixa up the friends with the clients with Old Gosling.

The week of the party Versailles was at its peak. That is, my weeds were at the height of their beauty. My garden consisted of quack grass, burdock, pigweed, ragweed, crab, clover, and dandelion. It would have made quite a salad, but only Michael Field could ever pull it off.

My tulips, even after a spoonful of bone meal each, came up with their heads bigger than their bodies and lay right down on the table. I had to prop them up in a vase. They were *really* Sanpaku.

My starlings returned for their summer stay to find that I had closed off their hearth suite. This deterred them not one cheep. They went right to management and were assigned to the curlicue wood stands I had bought for $3 (installation and paint, $63). This necessitated acid baths once a week on the cement under the porch instead of the hearth scrubbing. Ah, well, at least the lice were on the outside looking in instead of on me looking out.

And, now, the oak began to shed its leaves, only

this time the shedding was accompanied by a strange chewing sound.

"Arnie, my oak is shedding and there's a chewing sound." I chewed and licked and swallowed. "I just can't afford to lose the oak."

"Now, don't you worry, go on out and pick up a leaf. Look at it carefully. I'll wait on you."

You bet he would. I meant nothing but money to Arnie. I rushed out and picked a leaf off the tree. It was like green lace. Its little veins had been carefully picked, the flesh of the leaf devoured.

I described the leaf to Arnie, and he said, "Well, just what I figured. The cinch bug."

"Poor old oak," I whispered. Another death knell in the front yard. "What can I do?" I begged.

"Well, the best thing to do is spray."

"Pray?"

"No, spray. Well, I guess you could pray, too, if you have a mind to."

"What is a cinch bug?"

"Well, it's a little feller that comes to our part of the country about this time of year."

"And eats trees?"

"No, just the leaves."

"Ah-hah."

"As I figure it, you're right off Route 6, aren't you?"

You'd think he hadn't dug my Inca princess wells and flown through the branches of my piss elm. "Yes, don't you remember, right off 6."

"Well, now, that's the very center of cinch-bug country."

Another terrific sales point to make when I wanted out of this nuthouse, or rather, bughouse.

"Don't they have any natural prey I could put around?" Don't think for a second I wasn't staying up at night studying natural prey.

Arnie thought a moment. "Yep, thrashers eat them and red-winged blackbirds, but it don't do no good. Why, one feller, a scientist, found two hundred cinch bugs in one thrasher's belly."

Thrashers, indeed! It had been hard enough to attract orioles. It was thanks to Clovis that I had the whole oriole population nesting in my trees. The hell with string! If you want golden orioles, buy a sheepdog and put her out in the sun. They swoop down and steal her hair. I found that they prefer the gray hair to mix with their twigs and grass. The olive-sided flycatchers like the white hair. Is there really any accounting for certain tastes?

At least, the lilies finally bloomed. They looked good but I knew I couldn't count on them. Surely to God if they were decent on top, the mice or the moles or some pest was slowly chewing away at the bottom. Probably, the day before the party, they would all fall out and leave the garden bald.

The thing to do was pop for potted plants, keep the lights dim and the drinks coming, and pray for decent weather. As they say in Old Gosling, I was as busy as an old yellow jacket in a bed of hollyhocks.

I asked the three worker-friends I owned as guests for the weekend. I kidded them not. Peter wanted to know if he should bring a suit, or was he on bar with his white coat? Kit and Bob talked about nothing else but how good they were at cleaning up. They all got the point.

It rained, naturally, on the first, and it rained, naturally, on the second. Both days should have gone toward fixing up the terrace and lawn, but all we accomplished was a lot of cooking. In fact, I hadn't figured on the four-day weekend when I planned my garbage. Everything has been written about how to live graciously, but no one other than Phyllis Diller has ever coped with garbage. (She's right, just put it in the freezer.) I called up the Toss It Garbage Disposal Service.

"Good morning. Toss It." I certainly would not like to be that operator with a hangover.

"Is Mr. Toss in?"

With a voice that spelled out boredom, she pointed out, "This is the Toss It Disposal Service."

"This is Miss Trahey. I subscribe to your service." I somehow sounded like I was from the *Ladies' Home Journal* and wanted to interview her. "Look, I want to see about an extra pickup tomorrow."

And then I went off on one of those unexplainable, long-winded dissertations about how I was giving a lawn party and I was up to my ears in garbage, etc., etc. I had inherited this trick from my mother who used to explain to waiters—all waiters—

why she couldn't eat asparagus. (Believe me, neither Toss It nor Mama's waiters gave a tinker's damn.)

"Just one moment, please, I'll connect you with our unit manager."

A unit manager in garbage, fancy that! Did he sort it or count it?

"Murdock speaking."

I went through my whole tale of woe again.

"Gosh, miss," he said, "I'm terribly sorry, but we're so short of help this weekend, I don't think we can help. With the holiday and all."

"It's vital. It's imperative!" Again I described how I was up to my ears. By Tuesday, I'd be gone. I was getting nowhere and I knew it. Then I decided to play Yankee. I'd learned a few tricks in Old Gosling.

"Mr. Murdock, if you don't pick it up, I'm going to phone around until I find a service that will. And whoever picks it up this week, picks it up for the other fifty-one."

Before coming to Gosling, I had no idea that garbage collectors were so numerous and so highly competitive. I had even heard of one that was giving plaid stamps for every load.

"Well, let me put it this way," he said with oil on his watery voice. "If we can, we will."

"Well, let me put it this way. If you don't, you don't ever again."

As I had been speaking, I noticed a pile of sawdust beginning to accumulate at my feet. It was definitely coming from one of the beams—a beam, I might add, on which the house rested. I ran for Peter.

"Pete, my God, the house will be gone before the party. Just come look."

"I don't think that's so serious," he said as he sifted through the sawdust. "I don't think you ever see the work of termites. One day the house falls down and that's that, but you don't know what they're up to. You sure know what's going on here."

"Oh, what do you know, living in a cement house with pilasters in the East River?"

I called the Ace Pest Control.

"Well, lady, what's the trouble?"

I could have read him a list, but I confined myself to the present and most urgent subject.

"I'm sure I have termites." I told him exactly what was happening. I was an eyewitness to the pile that kept heaping up right in front of my foot.

"Don't sound like termites. Termites eat sawdust. They don't make it."

"What could it be? They're chewing up the house." I now did my imitation of these bugs.

"Those are carpenters ants from the way you're describing them. Just get some bug spray and let 'em have it."

"Okay, get the mariner's horn," I shouted to Peter. "Hornblower strikes!"

They all came out, hundreds of them, with their little saws in their dead noses.

"We'll eat at the Inn tonight. I have saved the house."

"First, let's go to the store and buy some kind of lights for the driveway. Otherwise, you're going to have to have a tow truck on hand to get people out of the mud." A cheerful word from Bob who had been out trying to figure a way to park cars.

I didn't want to spend $9.95 for ten hurricane lamps to stick in the ground all the way up the road, but towing clients' Ferraris out of the mud was no way to endear them to our ad agency. Mrs. Jean Paul Getty charged the hurricane lamps, stuck them in their proper places, filled them with kerosene, and went on to bigger and better chores.

The Fourth was a beautiful day. The ground was still damp and yukky, but if the ladies didn't wear shoes with too skinny a heel, they would be able to stay on top and not sink in too far. Most people I knew would stand hip deep in water for a lot of free Scotch.

We couldn't get it through to Orville that he, my closest neighbor, hadn't been invited. He was in and out all day, except during the Veteran's Parade. However, he came down immediately after in his uniform, beret, and boots to show us how to fold the flag. Each time we folded it Orville smelled more like the Christian Brother who's in charge of the sherry output.

I had developed a trick with Orville that usually worked. The minute he'd arrive I'd hop in the car to go to the store. After six trips down the driveway, Kit was getting peeved. "Every time I have something ready to put in the fridge, Orv arrives and we have to go bye-bye."

"Would you rather take the flag down and fold it?" Peter asked. For my money, a trip down the road was a cheap price to avoid a treatise on Apache arrowheads.

Finally, the first guest car arrived. I unsuccessfully tried to chuck Orville. It was the Mintons, with Lucy in a flowered chiffon dress and spiky shoes. "Bye-bye, Lucy," I thought.

Mr. Minton seemed surprised to see a Commando at the party, but I figured, what the hell, let the Mintons learn how to fold a flag.

As with all Fourth of July bashes, at least a third of the guests were ones I didn't know. Everybody brought a body or two or three who were *his* houseguests.

Peter gave me a nudge and said, "Here come two chic-ies."

Two men wearing dark green slacks and white short-sleeve sports shirts appeared. I thought maybe they were twins. But the party was swinging now, and I could hardly do more than invite them in, give them a drink, and introduce them to the nearest group. Then they would be on their own.

"Hello," I said warmly, coming on like Tracy in *The Philadelphia Story.* "Do come in and make yourself at home. It's casual. Just go to the bar and take what you like." As I started to introduce them around, I asked them their names. The one chap seemed bolder than the other.

"Harris is my name. This is Jenkins." No first names. Well, I used "Mr." and took them around.

As I led them away from Lucy Minton, Harris whispered, "Lady, we're from Toss It."

"Oh, the garbage!" I had forgotten.

They smiled sheepishly, "I'm afraid we're late. You're our last call, but Murdock said it was an emergency."

Lucy Minton had liked Harris and headed toward him again. I shepherded him right into the kitchen. Hopefully, she'd get stuck in the mud and be slower.

"Maybe you can carry the cans up through the house, since everyone is outside." We were in luck. The only person we met was Mr. Huggins, my men's-shoes client who had been to the john upstairs. He looked surprised, but then he always looked surprised.

As it got dark, Bob turned on the lights and lit the hurricanes. People came and went. It was a good party; everyone seemed to be having fun.

Then I heard the Old Gosling Fire Department coming hell-bent up Old Gosling Road. They hadn't bought a siren yet, so some man banged on a pan—at least it sounded like that.

"Must be a fire." Minton said.

"Oh, it's just some firecrackers or a sparkler or two."

The sounds got closer and closer. It was a very close

firecracker. Minton walked around the house looking for sparks. "It can't be anything, Morris," I
shouted. "The house is too soaked to light up."

"Sounds like they're out front."

They *were* out front. Peter came running. "You
had better come—the fire engine is in the front
yard."

I raced up and peered down the road. It was dark
as a dungeon. Only the headlights of the fire truck
were to be seen. However, in the dim light I could
see the fire chief shouting at Orville Henderson.

"Where is it, Orville? You put the alarm in."

"Put the goddamned thing out myself waiting for
you! You and your fancy equipment," he panted.

I looked in amazement at what was left of my hurricane stuck-in-the-ground lamps. Orville was jumping up and down on the last of them, his Commando
shoes burned to charcoal.

"Why, your whole place would have caught in a
minute with the way it was raging. Up and down this
road. It had caught everywhere." He said this
proudly, a mad Manischewitz glint in his eye. (He
had switched brands.) He did a salute, turned on his
heel, and passed out.

The fire chief was sympathetic. "Guess he thought
it was a forest fire."

I could hear Lucy and Morris Minton calling,
"Could we help?"

"No, nothing serious, be back in a sec," Pete
called. We dragged Orville to his porch. The fire

truck drove off with a promise that I could buy some tickets to their carnival.

I didn't say a word, but Ruth must have chewed Orville out. He didn't come near me for the rest of the summer. That was worth at least ten hurricane lamps.

X

With the party out of the way, I settled down to enjoy the privacy of the barn. Hidden from the road, fence-surrounded, and my only neighbor now off limits, I believed I was safe. But, in the country, once your mailbox gets the mark of sucker on it, you are bound to have the Saturday solicitors.

The rabbit-toothed girl came wanting to know what I'd do in case of nuclear warfare.

"Clear out," I assured her intelligently.

"You can't. The vegetation goes." Obviously she had been trained.

"Die, I guess."

Her eyes teared up. "You don't have to. Your Civil Defense will help. Do you have a bomb shelter built or in mind?"

"This whole place *is* a bomb shelter," I assured her.

She marked it down and left. So much for survival in Old Gosling.

The Boy Scouts came with lightbulbs and the Girl Scouts with stale cookies. The Jehovah's Witnesses brought their little square-headed children and the Bible several times. (They had a passage specially marked for me.) The man from the Blind Institute came with potholders the blind had never touched, and a young man came all the way from

Bridgeport for a donation to the Bridgeport Diocese.

"What do you use the money for?"

No one had ever asked him. He had to go to the car. In the glove compartment was his list.

"Well," he said, "fifty dollars will buy a painting for the convent waiting room."

I am not an aficionado of Church painting, not since Hieronymus Bosch turned in his brushes. "Nope, no paintings."

The sallow-faced, hollow-cheeked man looked uncomfortable. You were supposed to just give the money and let him and the big Bishop spend it. Well, tough! Let little sallow-face work for his money.

"Well, for sixty-five dollars you could put name plaques on the priests' doors."

Now, I wouldn't have minded putting *my* name plaque for sixty-five dollars on every door of the novitiate. But if the big brothers couldn't find their own rooms without a nameplate, the whole venture seemed pretty silly, anyway.

I assured him if he could come up with something that I liked, I'd buy. It crossed my mind that the only thing they didn't have on the sheet was a skull for the refectory table—*that* I'd buy. Now, of course, I know there's a black cross on my mailbox that only the diocesans see.

I was sound asleep one afternoon in my backyard with Clovis curled up in my arms protecting me, when I heard a voice far, far away babbling on. Slowly, consciousness trickled through.

"I'm terribly sorry, but I rang the bell and no one answered. Remember me, I was at your fireman's benefit." She giggled.

Clovis woke and was so frightened at the shadow cast on us that she fled into the peony bed. I tried to calm her down. Excitement like this was bad for her high blood pressure. The book I had been reading fell to the grass, and I pulled myself up into a sitting position.

"My name is Alice Shaw, but everyone calls me Alcy. We came with Affie and Toni to your party. Remember?" Of course I remembered: she was in the half of the guests I never met.

"Sit down," I mumbled. Then I realized unless she curled up in my arms like Clovis did, there wasn't anywhere for her. She looked around quizzically.

"Here, I'll get a chair."

She picked up my book and called, "Good book."

She had that nasal Bennington sound—a real tooth clencher if ever I met one.

"Obviously exciting," I replied. "Just see what it did for me."

"Buffsey loves Bond. Buffsey's my mate."

"Really."

"That's why I'm here."

"Buffsey or Bondsy?"

"That's what everyone said, you'd be just a perfect neighbor. I think you are going to be perfect, too."

I didn't know whether she meant I'd share sugar

and flour with her, or whether she was casting *Tosca* for the Old Gosling Workshop. I did know I had not been wrong in avoiding the natives.

"Would you like some coffee or a drink?"

"Oh, it's too early for drinksies."

With her around, it would never be too early. She sat across from me at the kitchen table and we chatted about Old G. She chatted as well as her clenched teeth could chatter. Sometimes it became so mixed up—the clench and the words—that she literally had to press her teeth up with her tongue. She was real Sandy Dennis material.

"Buffsey's mad. They want to zone this stretch of Old Gosling Road for light industry and, he says, ruin it. We live right down from you." So she belonged to that red covered-wagon mailbox.

"Light industry. How marvelous. Don't forget," I said bitterly, "it could be heavy industry."

"You're joking."

"Yes, I am joking, but I haven't had much success at Town Hall."

She whispered to me, although there wasn't a soul around except Clovis chewing on a peony. "Buffsey says that—he's a lawyer—the merchants are just ruining Old Gosling." Her baby-blue eyes swam with tears.

"Well, I'm game. What do you think you can do about it?" I had fought twice that year. Once with SNET, the Southern New England you-know-what. They had challenged the height of four of my trees. I suggested they hang their wires higher; they suggested I get my trees lower. They won. Then I had fought with the power company about taking down five lovely old two-hundred-year-old trees along the highway. They were on the part of my property when I paid taxes, but were on the state's five feet when they wanted to hack them down.

I had at the fourth set of characters who had arrived to get my permission. "Who wouldn't rather look at some nice power lines than five old trees? You gotta be crazy, man."

"Well, lady, we're stringing high power lines to the new Benrus plant, and those trees are definitely in the way." The ironic part was they made it clear that they would take them down, permission or not, and I wondered why they asked in the first place. To make me happy with another utility company, I guess. After much screaming and letters to the press, I had my choice of six new pines or three willows.

Benrus wouldn't give me the time of day, so I could see little point in Buffsey's or Alcy's chance with the industrial zoning. "You can't win here, Alcy. They have the time, the money, the lawyers. I can't get up here every Tuesday to fight the regular zoning petitions."

"Never say die," Alcy said bravely. Well, she had the time and the tears. Maybe it would work. She also had a lawyer for a husband. That couldn't do anything but help.

"Okay, give me what you want signed and I'll pay my part."

"I just knew you'd be right people. Buffsey is giving a drinking pow next Saturday. Can you and that sweet man come?" I assumed she meant Peter, although with Buffsey, she might have been hung up on Harris or Jenkins.

"We're going to a party next Saturday night at Lily Bofford's. She's a friend of Peter's," I said, hoping to lose Alcy forever.

"Lily and Pat Bofford? Smash! We'll be there after. They're having an eleven."

Whatever that was, I forgot it. Old Gosling was becoming much too social for my blood. Suddenly from out of the peony bed, Clovis ran dancing, screaming, and hopping.

"Isn't she cute?" Alcy clapped her hands.

I flew out, knowing full well that Clovis must be in the throes of death. She had never jumped in her life. She had distemper, I was sure. She flung herself into the house, moaning and groaning.

"Alcy, something terrible is wrong with her." I was frightened. Alcy copped right out and left with her petition and, "Well, see you at the Boffs."

I immediately took Clovis to Dr. Mann. It wasn't easy, since she writhed and cried. I wore my mittens so that if she bit me, I wouldn't get distemper, too. I most certainly don't want to die barking.

Dr. Mann immediately gave her a shot to quiet her down. I then waited in the waiting room with the rest of the pet slaves. I must have looked odd in my mittens and shorts, since one little old man wanted to know if I was the lady with the Falcon.

It was my turn and Clovis was much better now.

Dr. Mann ran his long thoughtful fingers through her mane. "Nope, nothing here. Nope, nothing here. Nope, nothing here." As he pulled up her head to stare in at her gums, he made his usual ugly remark, "Undershot jaw."

"You've never seen anything like it. She just flew into the air screaming," I babbled on, a distraught mother whose baby needed instant surgery.

"Well, I think a bee probably stung her. She'll live." He had the audacity to smile; he was probably laughing when the *Graf Zeppelin* went down in flames.

I packed Clovis up and took her home. She was sound asleep when I got there and I tucked her in her bed—correction, my bed—where she snored loudly all afternoon. Poor baby, no wonder: what a morning! I wondered which had been a greater shock to *my* system: Alcy or Clovis. I was soon to know.

"Frankly, Pete, I don't want to go to a party."

"Oh, for heaven's sake, you're going to turn into an aster sitting here. It's good for you to get out and see someone in Old Gosling besides the butcher, the baker, and Orville Henderson."

"I came to the country to get away from people and relax. And, besides, I won't like them. Alcy, Buffsey's wife, said they were adorable."

"Screw Alcy, whoever she is. They really *live* in Old Gosling. Don't even have a pad in town. And they know everyone. He's a terrific painter and she makes fab enameled jewelry."

"Sells at Alexander's!"

"The hell it does, it's all in museums."

"Okay, let's go."

Lily and Pat had converted an old stable into an old stable. They had not wanted to lose any of the stable artifacts and they hadn't. Sandy should see this. They had lost none of the horse and barn charm. It still smelled of manure. Lily, a fat dumpling of a woman, showed me the bar which was, she said, the cleverest thing Pat had done.

"See, these were all stalls for horses."

"Heavens!"

"And Pat decided to let it be the bar. Pat says the cocktail hour is his quiet hour, and he likes to be alone. No people. So we left all the stall walls up, and you and Peter will drink in Number 3. Pat drinks in Number 1, and he is really fussy about not having joiners."

"Heavens," I said, "I wouldn't go in there for all the vodka in Moscow."

Between Mercy and Heaven, I got through the tour. I was "admiring" a painting I wouldn't bore Clovis with. Lily said, "Yes, we love that Flink."

"It's terribly colorful."

"Pat thinks it's Flink's best. You like painting?"

"Yes, very much."

"Oh, Pat will love you. He's a good painter. Quite good, I think. He's all involved now with a turnip."

"Heavens."

I kept hoping Pete would rescue me, but he didn't. I could hear him out on the terrace with someone saying "Mahvelous" a lot. The phony! Of course, there I was inside, saying "Mercy."

"We're having an eleven tonight."

"Oh."

"Pat likes people to come at eleven. That is, people people—you're not people people. He likes to just have your kind for drinks, quiet drinks, then din-din, and then at eleven he loves people people. That's because Pat says he turns into a person at midnight. Right after dinner, if you ask him nicely, Pat will show you and Peter-baby his new paintings."

I didn't ask. I made the usual offer about helping Lily in the kitchen, but she said it was all done. At that moment she was straining bananas.

"We're having real Suez curry tonight. Pat got the recipe when he was in Suez. He imports the real curry. It's hot. It's supposed to have a terrific effect on you sexually."

"Mercy. I didn't know you put bananas in your sex." I had meant curry. Lily screamed with laughter. "Wait till I tell Pat that."

"Better wait till din-din, or he'll be angry."

I made up my mind I would concentrate on the salad and the rice. During the stall hour, Lily popped in now and then to see if we were enjoying ourselves.

"We could have stayed home and watched the movie," I said to Pete. "Just the two of us, cozy as bugs."

"Everybody happy?"

"Everybody happy," came the chorus from the various stalls.

I looked at Pete with a cocked right eye. He got the message. "Just shut up now and live through it. When I think of the squares you've given me this year, Lily and Pat are like an evening with Liz and Burton." He was partially right. No, he was totally right.

After dinner the Lord and Master appeared, quite smashed. He was tall and slender with huge green eyes, long red lashes, red eyebrows, and a Harris-tweed beard. He wore jeans cut off at the knees. They had been patched and washed so many times, I could only hope they'd make it through dinner.

The curry was so hot that it burned the outside of my mouth before I even gave it a crack at my tongue. And sake was no way to wash it down. There was an avocado mess and no rice. Well, I thought, push it around.

We went immediately to the loft after dinner. It was a huge white room with gallery lights, no chairs, cushions, and plenty of paintings. Pat had yet to utter a word. I wondered if he was a mute. It was like Pete not to tell me something like that.

But Pat didn't need conversation. He had Lily. She took over and the show began. It seemed that Pat only owned one spare frame, so that for each painting he showed us for our appreciable ohs and ahs, he also held the frame up around it. It was a two-handed feat, like double-handed chocolate dipping.

"This is 'Spinach,' " Lily called. Some of the other

guests, the Stall 4 pair, were talking. " 'Spinach,' "
she underlined. They quieted down.

"Oh, Pat, that is a dream," Lily said. "I didn't understand this at first," she reassured those of us with
our mouths open, "but the more I see it the more
'spinachy' I feel. Biennale, Pat. Pure Biennale."

Pat waited for my reaction, which at that second
was to leap up, take off all my clothes, and writhe on
the floor (I had heartburn) .

"Great color."

We went through "Pure," "Meaningful," "Whim-
sical," "Miracle," "Deep," "Pensive," and "Fab."

Lily decided to tuck her dress in her bloomers and
stand on her head. "Digestive," she mouthed at us
upside down. So I wasn't alone with my desire for relief. Her skirts kept falling and she kept tucking,
which was pretty damned good exercise for a lady
that size.

I could have killed Peter. He kept saying, "Just
the thing for your white wall."

"Oh, heavens, I couldn't afford anything as good
as that."

A mistake. Lily was up on her pins in a second.

"A lot of our good friends can't afford a Pat, but
they give him little-bitty sums every month for
years, and before they know it, they have a Pat of
their very own."

The curry was afire now. I asked if Lily had any
Alka-Seltzer or Maalox. Pat looked at me like I had
slapped her full in the face. "Oh, it was delicious, my
ulcer is kicking up."

If I had spelled out this lie it couldn't have been more obvious. But they did not have anything. Lily suggested I stand on my head, but I knew better. Pat would have a new carpet called "Curry."

Pete went for a breath of air, leaving me behind with the final *pièce de résistance*. It was a triptych that was a complete counter from the automat. It had Jell-O with whipped cream, custard, lemon pie, apple pie, blueberry pie, chocolate layer cake, white cake, angel cake, applesauce cake, and fruit salad—in fact, every imaginable dessert one could ever think of behind the slots.

It was so incredible, I gasped, "My God!"

This set Pat and Lily off to laughing. They cried. They slapped each other. Lily finally controlled herself enough to say, "HHhhhhhheeeeee, what . . . that's what everyone . . . body . . . heeeeeeee . . . says!"

The exhibit was over. I thanked Pat for showing me his work. It was just eleven o'clock. I wanted to go home to my clean, antique-filled barn. The eleven was just beginning in the stalls.

Lily said, "Maidie Jones is coming. She has a house on Whipstick Road."

"Who is Maidie Jones?"

"Why, darling, she's the hottest property Herman Fry has. 'Sing on.' 'Chou Chou.' 'What a Wonderful Ranch.' "

"Oh, yes, of course." I knew the sounds of the songs, but I sure didn't know Maidie or Herman.

"Winnie Wynant is coming. She's just behind the Inn."

I took a chance. "She writes."

"Of course, *My God Is Not an Ark At All.*"

There was a steady stream of arrivés. Two boys. Two girls. Two more boys. A bearded ape with a pregnant wife. Five dogs. Pete introduced me to Jim-Jim and Frank.

"They're Gothic."

"They're what?" I said crossly.

"They write spooky stories."

A few faces familiar from supermarket shopping appeared, and then Alcy and Buffsey arrived in their linen Bermudas. *Matching* linen Bermudas. She hugged me. Buffsey hugged me. They were delighted I was really socializing in Old Gosling.

Then Maidie came: toreador pants, high backless shoes, bracelets. She seemed pleasant enough, with a vacant right eye. Her agent was with her, an intense balding man who brought her drinks and scolded her about eating cheese.

"You know what cheese does, Maidie. Naughty, naughty. Ties her up in knots," he explained to me.

After Maidie had a couple of straight vodkas she got bored, sat bolt upright, grabbed the edge of her chair, kicked her feet to and fro, and sang a number from her vast repertoire. As she drank more and more, her voice (which was high anyway) reached new hair-raising pitches.

Winifred Wynant arrived wearing a tight yellow

sweater and black cord trousers grounded into chukka boots. She had a stomachache and sat staring into her Fernet Branca. She spoke to no one.

Suddenly, there was a large crash. Pat was juggling three soda bottles and missing every third one.

"Put on your sandals, honey, if you're going to make glass floors," Lily said. "He's so naughty when he's happy. It's his turnip that's going so well."

Pat obediently put his sandals on and resumed his bottle work. He lost the center ring, however, when Lynn and Lou—the two girls—had a fight over whether male designers really hated women. Lynn slammed out of the house and Lou had another drink while she smoldered. We heard a great crash and Lou flew out. Everyone tried not to listen, but there was not a sound. Then *Pat* was missing, and this made Lily nervous. Maidie had gone to sleep. Lily went off with Winifred to find Pat. When Pat came back he couldn't find Lily. This made him mad. Two of the boys who hadn't come together had gone off together, leaving two wretched mates consoling each other.

When for the last time I threatened to make everything that had happened seem like silent movies, Peter finally said okay, we'd go.

There was my barn, all quiet and sleepy. There was my watchdog, all sleepy and quiet. There was a moon. Pete fixed us a drink. We sat on the $400 retaining wall. I asked him to get a chair off the $500 lawn and to put the $10 light off on the $300 gravel path.

"Pete, do you honestly enjoy that sort of thing?"

"Hell, no, but why not?"

"Because I don't come to the country for that city atmosphere." No, the Old Gosling social set wasn't for me. I preferred Orville and Ruth, Arnie and Mrs. Firenza. Maybe I was just feeling pretty good for an old lady.

XI

So far I had managed to keep Versailles as my private retreat. But if you're in the ad-agency business, you are bound to have clients. Let's put it this way—if you don't, you're in trouble. We had done very well with the Native Herring account, but now their man in New York was being sent back to Holland. Before they would choose a replacement, Else Runing, the owner who lived in Amsterdam, was arriving to look over the possibilities. Hopefully, we would be sufficiently pleasing to her so that even with a new man, we would get to keep Native Herring as an account.

Though I had written to Else, I had never seen her. True, she hadn't seen me either, but she had seen our herring advertisements and liked our herring radio commercials. Well, since she was planning to arrive on a Friday evening, I wrote and asked if she'd like to spend the weekend with me in the country. She liked.

I wanted the barn to look in tip-top shape, so I consulted Mrs. Firenza. There was no use trying to hire anyone to do floor scrubbing, waxing, or to wash the big windows if there was a Cousin Firenza in the business.

"Nobody I know has gotta machine. Look in da yellow pages. They good."

"Well, here's one on Old Post Road."

"What's his name?"

"Bruno Schneider," I read. Obviously the German colony was not her favorite.

"Dey pretty good workers," she allowed.

Mr. Schneider came over that very day, which in itself is unheard-of. The pattern in Old Gosling is four phone calls, one irate visit to the shop, a talk (pleasant and sad) with his wife or answering service before any workman worth his ego appears. Bruno was either an "alchy" or on his first job. He was also not what one would expect for a heavy worker. He was slightly built, about five feet tall, and weighed about 103 pounds I'd guess, with his overalls and pail. I also noticed that his suspenders holding up his coveralls were Ivy League. (Yale, perhaps?) He was clean, intelligent, and talkative.

"My goodness," he chatted away, "what a surprise this house is."

"Why?" I steeled myself for the usual cracks.

"Well, it's simply adorable. From the road, you'd never know what it looked like. I love what you've done to it, and you have *the most beautiful rocks* I think I've ever seen." Well, needless to say, I adored Bruno Schneider.

"Oh, yes," I joked, "I have some of the most beautiful rocks in all of Connecticut."

He was deadly serious. "Oh, do you make a study of geology?"

I was flattered, but I answered honestly. "The only

study of rocks I have done so far is estimating the cost of removing them without blasting."

"Well, it's delightful. Simply delightful."

I would have eaten off Bruno's floor. I explained what had to be done. He understood, his price was reasonable, and he promised to finish it all within the week.

"You have a deal," I said.

"Oh, incidentally," he asked, "would you mind if I photographed some of your beautiful ferns and rocks? That's my hobby. Nature study. I'd do it when you weren't here."

So what could be wrong with his taking pictures of my rocks? If I'd trust him inside with my treasures, why not let him out with my rocks?

"Okay," I said jokingly, "but don't let it interfere with your real work."

"Oh, heavens," he said, "of course not. In fact, I'll take ten dollars off the bill just for the privilege of photographing. Such privacy here and back there in the woods. It's a veritable glen. And the rock, the big rock. It's simply magnificent."

He must be crackers, I thought. "Do you sell your pictures to *National Geographic* or do you do calendars?" I could see my rocks proudly displayed in the Connecticut Life Insurance Plan for the month of April.

"Well, it all depends. If I get some real beauties, I'll see that you get one."

Then I phoned Peter. "Peter, you'll love Else."

"Oh, yes, I can hardly wait to bite into that dish from the deep blue sea."

"I'm counting on you."

"Can she speak English?"

"Well, if she doesn't, it will be the quietest weekend we've ever spent."

"Well, who else?"

"Well, for Saturday night dinner I thought I'd invite Cher Valdin and Rodriguez." Cher was a dress designer who spoke French, German, Spanish, Yiddish, and Swahili. Rod was in the Finnish or Danish chair business. Someone was bound to establish contact with Else.

KLM might have oafs for stewardesses and smorgasbord for food, but it did one thing: it arrived on the dot. By the time we got to the terminal and dumped the car, Else had cleared customs and collected her baggage. It wasn't difficult to spot her. She was taller than anybody in the crowd and had a stiff-brushed blond hairdo that stood up straight, Congolese fashion. She had on a green paisley dress and long seventy-eight-button black gloves that seemed to go to her armpits and then some. From these endless Addams-family tubes, her hands emerged through slits in the palms, while the slinky black fingers were pushed up rakishly over the backs of her pale hands. She wore several silver bracelets over her gloves, and her hat was from a bullfight—a gaucho affair tied under her chin with a scarf.

"That's her."

"I knew it," said Peter, sighing.

"You are Else."

She smiled a deckle-edged smile, "Yah, yah, Else, yah, yah." She was obviously delighted to see us.

"This is Peter Carpenter, a friend of mine."

"Yah, yah."

"Do you have everything here?" I asked, anxious to get out of the airport and head for Old G.

She was going to stay for a while in our country, that was for sure. She had nine trunks, several pieces of hand luggage, and a shopping bag so huge you could fit The Hague's last tulip crop inside.

What with Clovis, Else, me, Peter, and Else's bags, we looked like we had just cleared out Emery Air Freight. Peter's car, which was only two inches off the ground, had me and the luggage in the back seat (or whatever that small shelf is). Peter and I cowered from the wind, but Else and Clovis sat upright and noble-looking, like they were the only two occupants of the car, Clovis driving and Else beside her.

Else loved the country. "Yah, yah, this is sooooo beautiful. Just like my country. Teeeepical Dutch, teepical."

The Merritt Highway was "teepical." Route 6 was "teepical." Old Gosling reminded her of Oosterschelde. Even my American barn reminded her of a lovely place in Alkmaar.

"Yah, yah, vuree nice. You come to my house in Meppel. I will show you teepical Dutch town. So beeutiful."

There was a definite chill to the air with fall coming. Else immediately slipped into a light summer frock for supper.

"Else, you'll be cold. It's cool here."

"Yah, yah, so nice. In Meppel it's much cooler this time of year. I am vuree warm now. Yes."

"Maybe you should take a sweater before we go downstairs."

"No, I don't unpack a sweater."

Peter was crushed up against a roaring fire he had built to take the chill off the room. We both had on sweaters, pants, socks. Else was content in her North-Sea-dotted Swiss.

She had several packages for me. It was that incredible minute when my instincts say "put the stuff away and forget it," but my hospitable side always wins and we open.

"Tomorrow, you rest. Else will cook teepical Dutch food like in Groningen, where I grew up. We will have Waterzooie. Beautiful. Delicious."

"How nice," Peter said.

"I bring my own grape soup, homemade schnapps, all the good things from my country. And for you I bring ancient family cookie mold." She drew out an oversize wooden cookie mold of a foot soldier with a feather cocked hat. It really was a beauty.

"Oh, Else, you should not have done all this. After all, you're my guest. Did people really make cookies this size?"

"Yah, in Holland, at Christmas, the Dutch are vuree good pastry makers. Yah. Vuree good."

Tomorrow, I thought, I'd make her a cookie for a

surprise. Else was tired and decided to turn in in high anticipation of National Dutch Day which she had declared for tomorrow.

Peter, after several thousand martinis had mellowed him, said, "She's quite a girl. Honestly."

"Oh, Pete, what would I do without you? You're a lamb to put up with all my chores."

"Oh, it's nothing—teepical of me, that's all."

I knew it was barely dawn because the birds hadn't started screaming yet. I went to the window to shut out the freezing air. It could not have been more than a fast forty out there. I couldn't believe my eyes. There on my lawn, obviously returning from the pond where she had had a dunk, was Else in a sunsuit, frisking about the lawn with Clovis snuffling behind. Clovis had obviously been tricked into swimming with Else. Else was pink and healthy; Clovis looked gray and cold.

As soon as Else got in her bath, I went down to dry Clovis. She was so grateful. "Dear God, you'll die of pneumonia. You must not go with that teepical nut."

I just made it up to the bedroom when I heard Else head for the kitchen again.

The rules of the house are thus: Get your own breakfast. I leave out the orange squeezer, set the coffee and the toaster. From then on out if someone is hungry, they work or go out. When I heard the fridge door opened for the thirteenth time, I thought, why fight it. Whatever Else wanted, she obviously hadn't found.

"Good morning, Else, how are you?"

"Gutten tag, gutten tag, I have had a swim in your pond. It's like the little Zeebrugge."

"Oh, grand. Weren't you cold?"

"Me cold, no, why cold? I swim till November in the North Sea." She was arranging lettuce on three plates. I didn't mind if she flew in Iranian caviar —*that* I can eat even for breakfast.

When Pete arrived, we went through the gutten-tag bit again. Pete was as stunned at her swim as I had been. I gave him a cup of coffee and took one for myself. Else screamed.

"Don't yet, drink nothing!" she cried. "Else brought surprise from the North Sea to American friends. Don't ruin taste buds with coffee!"

Peter had more guts than I and said, "Nope, drink now. Can't live without, regardless of North Sea surprises."

Else accepted Peter's wishes without a whimper. For me, I waited.

And then she took from the fridge, all wrapped in chopped ice, a long slab of hairy brown fish. Peter and I simply stared at her. This, thank heaven, she took as delighted surprise.

She held it up. "First catch yesterday, Juliana. Second catch, Else Runing."

She sharpened the knife before each slice. Then she lovingly lifted and placed a slice on the lettuce, then another. Each plate got three long hairy slices.

"Oh, Else, I'm allergic," Peter said. "Can't eat fish, get very sick."

She was disappointed. I was, too—I had just started to say that I was on a no-fish diet. Else wasn't happy but she cheered up by dividing his share between us. Winking at me, she said, "Vell, we get just that much more."

To say that the herring didn't sit well with me would be putting it mildly. Else ate her six slices, smacked her lips, and then lit into fried eggs. I tried to swallow it fast and not chew, but that meant gagging. I tried chewing it and adding lots of bread. For weeks, every time I hiccuped there was an echo of herring. It certainly didn't resemble the good de-haired stuff we advertised in sour cream.

Between dips in the pond, Else got her grape soup chilled and her huge stalks of asparagus cleaned. Should we serve the herring or save it for ourselves? I convinced her that she should share this delicacy with other gourmands. I painted Cher and Rod as herring worshipers.

Her Waterzooie smelled pretty good—that was some hope—and how bad could asparagus be? Just before dinner she arrived downstairs in a flimsy chiffon bearing a bottle and a box of chocolates.

"We have for cocktails. Vuree good. Teepical Dutch. Fockink and chocolate."

"I think most of my guests would rather have a gin, a Holland gin," I said hopefully.

"Yah, but good Fockink and chocolate is best, no?"

When Cher and Rod arrived, she lined us all up at the bar except Peter, who had run to the martini pot and started in without Else seeing him. Rat!

"Oh, what a shame. Can't mix drinks now, Else."
Canny rat.

"Now ve drink the Fockink like the Dutch." She lined up the glasses on the table and poured the Fockink to the very rim. "Now you put arms behind back, and person who empties glass on one sip is best man."

Well, there was a lot of snorting and choking. Guess who won best-man contest?

We all took a chocolate and hid it. Cher decided that she could switch to martinis. I decided I couldn't and fled to the kitchen and finished up my cookie mold. I had made the ready-mix cookie-mix earlier that day when Else was frolicking on the ice. I hoped she'd be surprised. I covered the cookie mold with the dough and popped it in the oven.

We had the grape soup and some Dutch gin. Then we had the asparagus spears. Else insisted we could and should eat asparagus like the Dutch. She picked up the entire spear with her fork and spoon, turned it in a split second in the direction of her mouth and without losing a rivulet of butter managed to eat the whole stalk. We watched. Cher, the stylish one, decided to try. Her asparagus collapsed midway between mouth and plate. With her marts and Fockink, I didn't think Cher would make it in any language.

"Jolly Green Giant eats his teepical American way," said the rat and cut into his asparagus with his knife.

Next came the Waterzooie. And then I heard a

strange squeak from the kitchen. I had the timer on, but thought I'd better check.

"See what's going on in the kitchen, will you, Pete, while I clear up a bit."

"Yah," he said.

Then I heard him whisper, "Sweetie, I have a surprise for you. Come on out."

As I arrived, the foot-soldier's foot was pushing the door open and heading out. The cookie was coming to life right before my eyes. Every second we stood there was a second lost. This foot soldier was no ordinary cookie. He was mean. A beast. And like Frankenstein's monster, he was going to come out of that oven to take over.

At last I summoned up enough courage to turn the oven off. But I was afraid to touch him.

"Take it out."

"I can't," I screamed. "I'm afraid it will grab me if I go anywhere near it. God knows how long it's been since this cookie's had a woman."

My hysteria in the kitchen had finally gotten to the rest of the dinner party. They all arrived to see what was going on. My soldier had both feet out and one hand. His cockaded hat was leaning on the back of the oven, his grotesque face leering beneath it.

"Else, it's your cookie mold, what should I do?"

"Gut Gott!" She shook her head. "In Holland, we should never make a cookie dot size. Dot's the biggest cookie I ever see, *anywhere*."

I shrugged. "It's nothing. That's just a teepical American cookie, Else, just teepical."

After scrubbing down Else's cockaded soldier and removing Fockink stains from every floor in the house, I decided that I was not a teepical advertising executive. The barn was for pleasure, not for business. I liked to know my muscles could unbend the moment Clovis and I got in the car and headed for the unpolluted air of Old G. No more clients on weekends. That was final.

However, I hadn't counted on having clients with a factory in Connecticut who wanted to drop by. Especially a brand-new account. Body Beautiful was my first bra and girdle account. Two middle-aged men ran the company. They were obviously fifty-fifty partners, as their office had a mental string tied down the middle of it. There were two identical desks, two identical lamps, two identical floor ashtrays (even though Mr. Fenschman didn't smoke), two air-conditioning units (even though one blew you through the doorway), two couches, two guest chairs, two phones, and two secretaries. The rug design must have been surveyed because the Oriental pattern was precisely cut in half where it should have been, in a good fifty-fifty arrangement. Mr. Fenschman had large buck teeth, wore silk monogrammed shirts, and gnawed on pencils. He was concerned with production and the factory. Mr.

Adams was of the Princeton school, smoked a pipe, wore Brooks Brothers suits, and seemed to be in charge of smooth sailing and buyer entertainment. The Body Beautiful line was designed by some girl with a game right leg whose show biz name was Mme. Sylvia.

Fenschman and Adams were extremely serious gentlemen who made a grand living out of their product. They were conservative. They made it quite clear that there was no nonsense in the Body Beautiful Company. They prided themselves on their product, which held up after ten washings. Their models stayed with them. Their designer stayed with them and Marshall Field & Co. stayed with them.

Mr. Fenschman had insisted that I see the important styles. "Come on over and get the feel of the line. You'll never know the feel of it until you see our Body Beautifuls on." He couldn't discuss a girdle without showing it to us on a model. His favorite was Dorothy, who had teased hair everywhere.

"Send Dorothy in," he rang on his intercom. It seemed there was never anyone on the end of the line when he called, and exasperated, he would go to the door and ask the secretary who had mysteriously returned to "please get Dorothy instantly." Actually, he never once made contact while I was there, and I thought maybe for Christmas I'd plug in the wire.

"Sid," he said to his partner, giving an Eberhard eraser a real chewing, "Sid, don't you think she should see 1021, 355, 1068, and 409?"

Sid agreed. "Why don't you show them the new item?"

Unfortunately, I had brought the art director with me and a copywriter who was quite apt to giggle. They made copious notes in an effort not to look at each other.

Mr. Fenschman looked shocked. "You think so, Sid? We haven't shown it to anyone, you know."

"Yes, so get a reaction, huh?"

Dorothy came in. Neither Mr. Fenschman nor Mr. Adams paid the slightest attention to her. She was wearing a little see-through housecoat and her feet were bare. She stood at attention.

"I'm not sure, Sid, until we show it to Emma Fiesler."

"She's the Croby-Flower resident. If Emma says good, it's fantastic. Fantastic," Mr. Adams explained.

Croby-Flower residents are not doctors. Each major group of stores in the country maintains a New York buying office with ladies who constantly scout the market looking for new things. As the expression goes, they are on the top of the market at all times.

"I don't see that it would hurt. They're part of the team now."

"Dorothy," Mr. Fenschman's buck teeth whistled out, "go in the workroom and tell Anna to give you the secret number. We should put a number on it, Sid, even if it's a secret. Then put it on and come back."

"The idea," Mr. Fenschman explained, "of this girdle is one that I have had in the back of my mind

for years. I've tried it, but it's never been successful.
Now I think I've got it licked."

"Does it have a name?"

"Tell them, Sid. It's Sid's idea."

"Well, it's a one-piece panty girdle and bra. Do
you wear a panty girdle?" he asked me.

I felt sort of embarrassed. Just the thought of dis-
cussing my underclothes with anyone left me that
way. Yet, it was silly because their approach was that
of a seasoned gynecologist.

"No, I don't wear a panty girdle."

"Too bad, you'd have more feeling for the garment," said Mr. Fenschman. I hoped our account
wasn't going to be jeopardized; business could be
lost for less than that.

"My wife wears one. She's been the nagging voice
in my head. Panty girdles are problems."

Dorothy had come in again and stood at attention.
She held her hands like a lieder singer and, finally
when Mr. Fenschman said, "Show," she dropped her
robe and stood at attention in her one-piece panty-
girdle combo. Mr. Fenschman, like a ballet master,
gave her a signal with his index finger, and she began
to pivot. It was the pivot of a zombie. She must have
figured out, or more likely Fenschman taught her,
that a full circle takes 360 counts. Each time she com-
pleted 60 counts she made a sixty-degree turn. Sixty
degrees again, another sixty degrees, until her front
faced you again.

"Now, you see for a woman who wears a one-piece

garment such as this, it is literally impossible to keep taking it off to have any normal functions," Sid explained.

"How true," I said.

"So we have come up with a construction in the crotch that enables her to have freedom. It emancipates her."

"Emancipates. That's a good word, Sid. A good word. Maybe that's what we should call it. What do you think?"

"Fantastic," I said.

"Terrific, Sid. We'll call it 'Fantastic.' "

"I thought you wanted to call it 'Emancipates.' "

Mr. Fenschman looked annoyed. "That's what I said."

"You said call it 'Fantastic.' "

"That's what she said."

Sid gave in as I figured he might. "Okay, let's call it 'Emancipates.' "

No one had turned Dorothy off, and she kept pivoting slowly, counting silently, showing off her 'Fantastic Emancipates.'

"What do you think?" It was my turn again.

"Wonderful."

"See, look here," he grabbed Dorothy's leg. I knew he was going to show me the construction, and I quickly tried to distract him.

"It's an old Indian principle, the way the cloth is crossed, isn't it?"

"Preeee-cisely. She caught on, Sid."

I felt relieved, if not proud of my quick thinking. If I had had to look at Dorothy's construction, I would have collapsed. Since Mr. Fenschman had put Dorothy's leg down, she had started pivoting again.

"Well, now, let's get down to work. Next week is the big showing," Fenschman said. "We have it right at the plant and our head designer will be there."

"When is it?" I asked.

"Let's see, Sid, when is it?"

"On the sixteenth."

"On the sixteenth, that's a Friday. Can you spend the day?"

"Sure, Friday is fine. I go up to Connecticut anyway. I'll just pack up my dog and we'll drive right on up from your factory."

"You live in Connecticut?" Mr. Fenschman was enchanted. "Sid, she lives in Connecticut." I felt this almost evened the score of my not wearing a panty girdle.

Sid, too, showed great interest. "Whereabout?"

"In Old Gosling."

"Sid, that's not far from where you are, is it? What is it, Sid, about twelve miles?"

Mr. Adams said, "It's about twelve miles."

"What do you have, a house?"

"No, I have an old barn."

"Sid, she has an old barn. That's interesting!"

"I've been converting it."

"Sid, she's been converting it."

I was getting used to the fact that despite Sid's presence, Mr. Fenschman was his translator.

"My wife loves old barns. Maybe you'd show it to her."

Well, I hadn't been in the ad business all these years without learning my lesson. "I'd love to show it to her."

"When?" Mr. Fenschman hadn't been in the selling business all these years without learning his lesson—he wanted a signature on the order.

"Well, will your wife be at the showing?"

"Of course, she'll be there and Sid's wife, too."

"Well, why don't you come and have a drink after the showing. You'll be tired."

"Wonderful. Sid, does Nancy like barns? Laurie loves them."

"Sure, we'll come." Nancy could hate barns for all Sid cared.

The following Friday, the Body Beautiful Showing for Fall was held according to schedule in Connecticut at their new modern air-conditioned plant. Body Beautiful had done their utmost to keep the spirit of Old Connecticut by doing the facade of their plant in Early American Post Office. This, plus a shuttered door and a lawn, were most assuredly enough to shut up their neighbors. It was unreasonable for people who lived around Body Beautiful to resent the thousand-car parking lot, the traffic lights, the traffic twice a day, the grim fencing, the sound of machinery, the constant shipping, and the sign "Body Beautiful" that glowed in the dark—a neon nude girl bending to and fro.

Body Beautiful buyers and the press were driven up by air-conditioned bus for a picnic lunch on the Sound. They were wined and dined, delivered, gifted, and kissed. Each buyer received a giant jug of Body Beautiful Bath Oil (a new Fenschman-Adams enterprise) : "If you wear it, your Body Beautiful will be more Beautiful."

Girdle buyers, for the most part, take their business as seriously as the manufacturers. They are all terrific advertisements for what the trade calls "Iron-maidens." Most of them are middle-aged or over and wear a size 44. They understand how to shove their own fat inside the Body Beautiful containers. Because of their size, they never embarrass any other fat customer in a fitting room who is having trouble shoving *her* fat around.

This Body Beautiful Show was given, so the invitation read, for the press. But the kind of press the girdle industry attracts—unless some murder takes place in a stretching machine—is confined to the girdle editors on fashion magazines and newspaper editors of women's pages. The magazine girls attend at the explicit orders of the publisher, who wants his pages of advertising each year. The newspaper ladies go because of their advertising directors. The top buyers seem to think they are getting special treatment at being let in on the press show. It's just the other way around. The press is let in with the top buyers. I knew neither the editors nor the buyers, except for Emma Fiesler, whom I had to kiss.

"Sid, introduce Emma Fiesler to Jane. Emma, this is our new agency lady. Here, kiss Emma, Jane. You and she will love each other."

A big juicy kiss went from me to Emma on her big juicy cheek. Kissing in the girdle market is as common as a twitch.

The gold chairs were out in the big showroom which accommodated about two hundred people. The showroom was French Impossible—a period thrust between Polish Renaissance and Italian Hopeless. It was off-white, pale green, and Fanny Farmer pink satin. Mme. Sylvia greeted the guests along with Fenschman and Adams. A few of the production men, in suits for the occasion, looking very nervous, helped seat the press and the buyers. They all had assigned seats, and Marshall Field was smack in front, as were *The New York Times, Vogue,* and *Bazaar.*

Two fat girls (way past their bunny days) appeared in one-piece pink and blue girdles and made the rounds. One had a tray of champagne, the other caviar. "Chamm-pain," the one in pink cried. "Calve-ier," the blue bunny coaxed. Obviously they worked in the plant. Probably Mr. Fenschman had put them on the Jell-O diet and paid for their permanents so they could be on tap.

When everyone was seated and had his champagne and ashtray located, Mme. Sylvia officially greeted us.

"Oim Mme. Sylvia. Greetings and selections"—

That was a new word—"from Mr. Fenschman, Mr. Adams, and the Body Beautiful Company. Isn't it a beautiful day for a Body Beautiful picnic?"

Applause.

"Today, as you see, I'm wearing famous Number 906, our fabulous lace all in one slip-bra, the number you can never not have on your shelves." (It was certainly resting comfortably on *her* shelves.)

"It's called, this new shade, 'Little Boy Beige,' because it gives you the little-boy look. That flat-chested Twiggy look."

On her it should have been called "Little Boy Bulge": Number 906 had never looked fuller.

"And here is our first number. It's called 'Night at the Opera.' " The pianist, a leftover from Liberace, played *Madame Butterfly* with plenty of arpeggios.

A jazzy blonde came out wearing a mink stole over her girdle.

Applause.

The gems on her ears and her neck and her wrists and her fingers sparkled in the showroom lights. On television she would have broken the tubes coast-to-coast. She dragged her mink stole and showed us all there was to know about that Night at the Opera. She emphasized everything that could be emphasized. She lovingly ran her fingers over her D cup, flattening her tummy, and Mae-West-like, stalked off the runway.

"*Vogue* called this one 'Diamond Circle.' Notice the garters are precious gems. These, of course, are by Harry Winston. Those we deliver, however, will be precious rhinestones."

The piano played "Diamonds Are a Girl's Best Friend."

"And here is Number 897, our famous 'Naughty Marietta,' which *you* have made our number-one best seller."

Applause.

At this point I noticed that the lady next to me, who was from the press, began to shake a lot. I couldn't remember whether she had sat on the *Town and Country* card or *Glamour* card, so I couldn't tell where she was from. She wore a huge big-brimmed hat and tried to hide her giggling behind it. She knew, as all editors know, that you don't antagonize the owner of a company that buys sixteen pages of advertising a year.

Then Dorothy, the counting zombie from the office, showed the climax of the show, "The Emancipation." Mr. Fenschman had been asked by Mme. Sylvia, who knew which side her girdle was buttered on, to give a commentary about the fabulous new fantastic emancipator. As Mr. Fenschman gave his speech, the editor cracked again and pretended she was choking. We were in direct line of Mr. Fenschman's gaze. I stared at him with unwavering eyes.

Applause.

"And now," said Mme. Sylvia, "for our finale. Here they come: Ava, Liz, and Mia. They bring you, along with the special Winston detective who guards these precious gems, one hun-dred and seven-teeee-fii-ahv thou-sand dollars' worth of gems. Mia, Ava, and Liz present" (piano: tum-tum-teee-tum) "Body Beautiful's 'My Bare Ladies.' "

Much applause.

Three of the heftiest ladies I had yet seen paraded out in new girdles, one peach-colored, one yellow, and one blue. "Daring? Yes!" said Mme. Sylvia, who thought any departure from white was wild.

The girls each carried a mask that was a photo mounted on a fan of the particular glamour girl they were impersonating. The lady at my left coughed so hard she had to leave the room. Obviously she didn't care whether she worked again or not.

"Ava's has a zip front for easy entry."

"And now for the final finaleeeeeeee." Mme. Sylvia was quite hysterical. "Body Beautiful presents Liz in our beautiful satin and Lastex one-piecer." Liz did her tour jeté. She wore, atop her satin and Lastex one-piecer, a floor-length wedding veil, and she carried a little bouquet of lilies of the valley. The applause was deafening. As she passed Emma Fiesler, she threw the bouquet to her just as practiced. Emma was delighted. If it worked for Emma, anything was possible.

Mme. Sylvia summed up her show. "Thank you for coming, have a wonderful, wonderful year." She was close to tears. Mr. Fenschman ended it with a toast to the new season, and the signal was given for the "bunnies" to start passing out more Moët-Chandon.

I flew into the ladies' room. The editor was leaning on a sink, crying. I took one look at her and all was lost. We screamed. We punched each other. We pounded the booths and exchanged "Little Boy Beige" remarks.

"Oh, God," she chortled, "I'll be fired for this, but did you see Ava?" And she was off again.

Emma Fiesler came in and I went out. Emma looked peeved as hell, and the editor went hurriedly into a stall. As I left, I heard Emma tisking at the editor and the editor screaming with laughter.

Mr. Fenschman was irritable as hell. "Sid, who was that broad that laughed through the show? Where was she from? *Town and Country* or where, because, by God, Sid, if you agree with me, I'm not going to give them a page of advertising. Do you hear?" He glowered at me.

"I don't think she was from either book."

"Sid, go get that card. Show Sid where you were sitting. Imagine laughing through our fall showing! I think she ruined the showing. I think so, Sid."

"So, Maury, calm down, you'll have to have a Gelusil if you keep it up." It was Mr. Fenschman's wife, Laurie, a small, frail blonde with a piping voice. "Sid, Maurice is all worked up. Tell Maurice to calm down." She worked on the Sid bit like Mr. Fenschman. I wondered how they communicated if one was missing.

Finally, we got Mr. Fenschman to the parking lot. The buyers were back on the bus and the doors of the Body Beautiful factory showroom locked. Mme.

Sylvia declined my invitation. I wondered if they had locked up the editor, as I never saw her again. For all I knew she might still be in the toilet laughing.

I agreed to lead the Fenschmans and Adamses home to my barn. After Clovis in the back seat of my car had been admired by all, she was kind enough to drool on Nancy's green silk linen. I started off Route 6, having given them explicit directions in case we got separated.

I landed home ahead of them. When I turned into the driveway, I noticed the lawn had been freshly cut, the flowers in bloom, the house painted, the shutters trimmed, the gravel weeded. All in all, I had a sense of pride now about the barn, like a teenage daughter the day the braces are removed.

Then it dawned on me that there was a car parked inside the fence. I knew it wasn't Mrs. Firenza's, and the liquor store had a truck. I went around the back. I walked down past the side of the barn and then I saw a pair of brown legs in lederhosen, but the head of the body was under the black cloth of a camera on stilts. It was Bruno Schneider, the floor polisher. That much was okay. But what Bruno Schneider was photographing was definitely not.

"My God, Mr. Schneider! What is that, the White Rock Girl?" There on Clovis Hill Rock lay a marvelously sexy nude, the kind seen on the foldouts of *Playboy*. She was lying face down and floating her hand in the ferns. When I came by, she was so surprised, she sat bolt upright. Now *she* was a natural for a Body Beautiful show!

I could hear Mr. Fenschman's car coming up the road. "Get her out of here this minute," I screamed at Bruno. "Get her out. Get her anywhere. I've got clients."

Bruno seemed annoyed by the interruption, but he definitely got the message. As I ran up the side steps to greet Fenschman and company, I tried to work out my next moves. I would let them in the upper-level front door. This way, Bruno and naked Nell could head for the downstairs bathroom where, I logically felt, she had left her clothes.

Nervously, I led my guests into the living room. They admired it. I knew I had to get them a drink. Problem: ice downstairs. "I'll go down and get some ice."

"We'll all go down. Laurie wants the dollar tour." Mr. Fenschman was in a much better mood now, and he thought this remark was so funny he repeated it for Sid. If he was so pleased with himself, I thought, wait till he gets a load of the main attraction on this tour. If he thought his Bare Lady act was naughty, wait'll he sees Baby White Rock.

Laurie's high voice was coming through. "Oh, this is simply lovely. Look, Maurice, we're on the ground floor."

The bottom floor of my barn is made of brick floors that run into the kitchen. The approach to the kitchen can be on either side of the dining room. Behind the kitchen is a storeroom complete with furnace and junk of the entire house. There is also a bathroom. Baby White Rock was either in the kitchen nude, in which case Laurie would see her first, or in the bathroom, in which case I could fail to show them the bathroom on the pretense that I forgot about the bathroom. Or she was in the storeroom, in which case Sid would probably see her first, as I had a feeling he would like storerooms.

"What kind of wood is that?" I was so nervous, I couldn't remember.

Laurie headed for the dining room again.

"Oh, did you see this?" I kept trying to get them to sit down. I was dragging out old photos of the barn before I bought it.

"Where is the icebox?" Mr. Fenschman asked. "You tell Laurie about the barn. She loves barns. She's in love with barns. I'll get the ice."

Mr. Fenschman found the fridge, and I heard him removing the ice.

"What's in here?" he called. Well, now, it was either the storeroom or the bathroom. I rushed past Laurie to see.

Mr. Fenschman opened the door to the storeroom and peered in. "Ah, a storeroom," he said. I took a deep breath, now that I knew that was clear. I called, "Mr. Adams, Mr. Adams, come down and see the storeroom."

That left only the bathroom downstairs. Laurie discovered that door. "What's this? A baby storeroom?"

This broke up Mr. Fenschman. "Sid, Laurie called the bathroom a baby storeroom."

We all laughed hysterically.

Then we all had drinks. Where in God's name could Bruno and his love have fled? Was it possible they had gone out the bathroom window when they heard us coming downstairs?

I prayed for the sound of a departing car, but my prayers were not answered. We had to do the upstairs sooner or later. I flew ahead in the hallway, almost knocking Nancy down. Mr. Fenschman said, "Watch it, Nancy. Watch it, Sid. Help Laurie watch it."

I cased the three bedrooms. Sure enough, on one bed was her complete wardrobe: slacks, shirt, shoes, and a Body Beautiful girdle. (Well, that was a point in her favor.) While I shoved my guests into another room, I hid her clothes. Then, when we went back downstairs, I wished to heaven I hadn't hidden them. Now if they went in upstairs, she wouldn't have *any* clothes to put on. I served another round of drinks and hurried back to put the clothes out. Then Nancy wanted to go to the bathroom, so I had to knock her over getting the clothes hidden again.

Mr. Fenschman said he was bushed. "We're going to have dinner, why don't you come. Sid, why shouldn't she come?"

I thought that one more nervous minute with Sid and Nancy and Mr. Fenschman and Laurie and I'd slit my jugular with a corset stay. I explained to them that the excitement of the show had really knocked me out, too, and I was due for dinner somewhere else.

"You'll get accustomed to the pace," Mr. Fenschman said, as he patted me on the back. "Sid, she'll get accustomed to the pace, won't she? Ha, ha, ha."

Sid nodded. Nancy nodded, Laurie nodded.

"We work hard, and we play hard, don't we, Sid?"

Nancy loved the barn—Sid said so. Laurie loved the barn—Mr. Fenschman said so. They left. As I watched the car finally go down the drive and turn on to the road, I raced back through the house. Bruno was nowhere. But his car was. I thanked God none of them had asked about it.

"Mr. Schneider?" I called. "Mr. Schneider, can you hear me?" My voice was uncontrolled rage.

I heard laughter, and finally from behind the Jesus Saves Rock (which is the biggest one I own) Bruno stuck his head out. I signaled and told him the coast was clear.

"I'm frightfully sorry," he apologized. "I thought you knew what a nature study was. I do hope I haven't inconvenienced you, but I didn't think you came up this early."

Miss White Rock sashayed across the lawn and finally emerged dressed. They both seemed highly indignant—like *I* was a dirty old lady.

"Perhaps I could work sometime when you're on vacation."

I merely pointed to the road. They got the point.

I had dreams that night of Clovis in the famous 906 cavorting around Mr. Fenschman, who had no clothes on at all. I thought it was the alarm clock for a while, and then I knew that it was the telephone.

"Hello," I said sleepily.

"Hey, Missa Tray, this Mrs. Firenza, how you?"

"Oh, fine, and you?"

"Oooooooooh me, pretty good for an old lady."

"What time is it?"

"It's ten o'clock, Missa Tray. You gonna sleep all day?"

"Never, not here in Old Gosling."

"You got everything okay in da house?"

"Yes, it looked fine to me. Why?"

"You don' notice da chest on da terrace, da big one?"

"No, I didn't."

"Well, somethin' is eatin' dat chest, Missa Tray."

"What could be eating it?" My old fear of termites returned. "Do you think it could be termites?"

"No, Missa Tray. Dat's a rat tooth."

"How do you know? It could be a chipmunk."

"Well, I'ma goin' tell you, Missa Tray, how Mrs. Firenza know. I caught a rat." She giggled proudly. "Yes, a *bigafata rat*. Oh, anna Missa Tray, you don't have to hire thatta man no more."

"Oh, okay." I didn't know what man, but she'd tell me soon enough.

"My cousin Vido, he's gotta da machine now, he come do your floors."

When I paid the Schneider bill, I took off the ten dollars he had promised me as a location fee. It would barely cover the cost of my giant bottle of Maalox.

It was in the fifth season that I kept trying to remember just what it was that had ever prompted me to buy the barn in the first place.

This was the year I had dowdy brown birds nesting in the rafters. They were phoebes, and their most charming trait was to scream "feeeeeeeeeeee-beeeeeeeeeeee" about 25,000 times a day. The first time I heard it, I was delighted. Then came the other 24,999 times . . .

But bird screams were no worse than the exploding sounds of creeping suburbia. There was hardly a week I didn't meet with Buffsey and Alcy over zoning or water-conservation lines or blinking traffic lights or screening laws for light industry.

This was accompanied every Saturday morning by the persistent high "nya-nya-nya" of a buzz saw. The man across the road was determined to cut down every tree on his land. When the racket stopped intermittently (I guess it meant Paul Bunyan was wiping the sweat from his pioneer brow), I would then hear his seven jolly kids, five dogs, and three cats at their round-robin contest of who could make the most noise.

On the other side of Route 6 I had the fun of hearing a teen-age band develop. Living across or down from doesn't matter one whit in this day and age of guitar amplifiers.

The Old Gosling police were sympathetic, but as long as the darlings quit before 11 P.M., there was not a thing they could do about electric zithers, bagpipes, guitars, or snare-drums. I knew better than to make a personal showing. Who needs rocks in the pool?

It was in the fifth season, too, that Clovis got ticks. Clovis was never much for the outdoors, living mostly behind the curtains in my bedroom or hugging the shower on hot days. Occasionally, when I wanted her to walk a bit (for fear she'd forget how), I would turn her out. Hurt and bewildered, she would head for Clovis Hill, her hair flying in the breeze where, instead of surveying her land and keeping a sharp eye out for poachers, she turned the other way around and studied the bottom of the rock.

Though I had found an occasional tick on Clovis, I never saw such a crop as this year. The evening I saw one quietly walking across my arm, I almost flipped. So it was in the fifth season that Clovis went to Dr. Mann for a tick bath. I was all for taking one, too.

"Do you think I'll get Rocky Mount Fever?" I knew I was being more concerned about my future at the moment than about Clovis.

"Haven't heard of a case in a long time."

"Well, let's clip her. Then we'll be sure she gets rid of them. It's better that way," I sobbed.

Thank heavens I had told him to leave her head alone. Of course, he had to have his crack: "Yes, with that jaw she'd look pretty bad." As they carted Clovis off to the guillotine, I patted her bravely and whispered, "He's got a wart on his nose."

I had never felt before that Dr. Mann and I had failed to communicate, but his idea of clipping and mine are quite different. By clip I mean clip. By clip he means shave. The fact is, I left a fat gray woolly sheepdog, contented, happy, cuddly. I picked up a skinny, high-strung, nervous pink wreck.

"What have you done with Clovis?" He had absconded with my trick dog.

"She'll get used to it."

But she didn't, and all through the fifth season until her hair began to show, Clovis had to have tranquilizers. Her summer was ruined, but it did give me a good excuse to omit people with dogs from my guest list.

There were some weekends when each soul I invited had to bring his dog. Those were the weekends it would have been better if I had bought a kennel rather than a barn.

When I traveled, Clovis wouldn't get out of the car, but when other people left home, Dinky or Rosebud or Muttsy were in great shape.

Cousin Sally called. She and John would love to come and see me, was it okay? Yes. Was it still okay if they brought Sheba? Yes. Did I know Sheba was in season? I don't know what would make them think that I knew—Sheba and I were certainly not confidantes. I reminded them that Clovis was a girl, and hung up.

Yet Sheba was by far the most remarkable of all the dogs I had ever entertained. She knew how to open the refrigerator door! Out she would trot to the kitchen, put her paw on the refrigerator easy-open pedal, and easy-open it with her nose. The door dreamed up for people with pans in their hands worked just as well for dogs with food on their minds.

"Can you believe it," Sally said proudly. "We have to keep *everything* in the freezer."

"Why don't you give her a good sock on the nose?"

Sally looked at me with hurt eyes. She was not sure that she and Sheba were welcome. "The remarkable thing is that now she won't eat anything we put on the floor at all. Ha, ha! We outwitted her. We just put her dinner on the second shelf, and she steals it."

"She steals her own dinner?" (*They* outwitted *her?*)

"Yes, it's the challenge and all."

"Why don't you give her a really good sock on the nose?" This time Sally was really hurt.

"Just because you have a rug for a dog, is that any reason why Sheba can't express herself?"

"Lord, no," I said. "Besides, I promised to get Clovis casters for Christmas. Then she can really get places."

Clovis would most certainly never open a fridge. In fact, if I didn't take her by the paw right to her dish, she would sometimes miss it by passing too far to the right or left.

Of course, no one came with his pet without a

weekend's sackload of dog chow. They might show up with nothing for themselves, but plenty for their babies.

With housepets for guests it was inevitable that there would be a stew of some obnoxious innards simmering away in a pot on Saturday morning. Then the slimy stuff was cut up into itsy-bitsy pieces for Irving or Hannah and left on the floor for them to chew on. The rest floated screnely in its grease in the fridge all weekend. If there's one thing I like to see first thing in the morning, it's a steer heart floating in guck next to the orange juice.

As for Clovis, she adored other dogs. She doesn't have a mean bone in her body. It was the other dogs that were mean. I realized this one weekend when Cher brought Frou Frou. Frou Frou is a foot-by-one-half-foot Maltese who literally pulled chunks out of Clovis. Each hour I would extract a large ball of Clovis' hair from Frou Frou's mouth, so that she wouldn't choke on it. Talk about circumstantial evidence!

Clovis thought this was jolly fun and would lift her elephantine paw to pat Frou Frou. Then Cher would scream, "Dear God, Frou Frou will be killed. Just look at what Clovis is doing."

I would show the hair hanging out of Frou Frou's mouth, but Clovis always came out looking like the bully.

One Sunday morning Frou Frou disappeared. Cher noticed that she was not within eye range and flung herself out of the hammock.

"Frou Frou."

No answer.

Clovis came lumbering out of the woods from behind her rock.

"You naughty dog, what have you done with Frou Frou?"

I must say this irritated me. What had Clovis done with Frou Frou? The fact that Clovis could still smile seemed like a miracle. Frou Frou had bitten her eleven times in two hours.

"She's around somewhere, you'll never lose that."

Cher was gone for an hour, and occasionally between the sounds of the teen-age band and the buzz saw, we heard the cry of "Frou Frou." Clovis had not moved a muscle to help. I can't say I blamed her.

When Peter came downstairs, I told him Frou Frou was missing.

"Well, come on. There'll be no peace until we find her. Maybe she's on the highway," Peter said hopefully. For two hours we searched for the dog.

As we headed back to the barn, an old Buick drew up alongside of us. "You looking for a dog?"

"Yes, a little white dog."

"How big?"

"So big."

They dug in the back seat and extracted Frou Frou. "We picked her up."

Even I was glad to see the rat. She promptly growled at me. I tucked her under my arm and let her spit all the way home.

The reunion with Cher was sickeningly performed, and Frou Frou's only thanks to me for finding her was to get under Clovis and bark, practically sending Clovis to dog heaven with fright.

But it seemed to me in this, my fifth season, that the dogs were no worse than the humans.

I had the Principessa. She was a friend of a client and she came from Milano. She spied all my old Good Will Italian wrecks of furniture, and tears came to her eyes.

"It's without doubt, that'sa my table from Asti Spumante."

"That's a table from the Good Will."

"Da Nazis stole everything, everya-thing."

So I was a Nazi. The Principessa decided that she was going to help with lunch.

"You let me make the salad? I make a Chesare."

"Okay," I said, "that's great. I'll slice up the chicken and you do the Caesar."

"Wonderful," she said. "Where do you keep the cleaned lettuce?"

I cleaned that lettuce up in a hurry.

"Now, mya dear, where is your crushed creeesp bacon?"

I made crushed crisp bacon.

"You have some lovelee toasted croutons, per-haps?" She was sitting down now, watching, like a bishop at mass with his altar boy. "I like, personally, to fry them in butter first, yes?"

"Oh, yes."

"Now I am ready for a coddled egg."

"Now I am ready to make it." Actually, I was ready for bed.

She was sensational, the Principessa, at tossing. With true Tuscan flair, she mixed the salad. All agreed that it was wonderful that a Principessa should be so down-to-earth.

Wally and Toni wanted to bring a friend.

"She's a doll, works for *Bazaar*."

"Doing what?"

"She's an editor."

"Does she know what we all look like? Does she know people are not talking about us?"

"Don't worry, Baba is a good sport."

Baba came from Oyster Bay and she was not a good sport—unless you could call her Olympian wardrobe changes a sport.

She appeared for breakfast in a Pucci shirt, Cleopatra sandals, Indian trousers, owl eyeshades. I was wearing a pair of blue-jean shorts and my pajama top.

She then changed to her sun jump suit and Sun Control Gelée.

She stayed in the sun for one hour. During that time she frosted her nails.

I asked her if she wanted to go to the store with me. She left for an hour and returned in linen shorts and a top from Greece. She was a big hit at the butcher's.

We returned home and she put on a new swimsuit. For lunch she returned to Pucci. Then more

sun, another outfit. I dreaded to think about cocktails.

"Isn't there someone we could call who dresses and
ask them, too?"

Sunday, she was really with it. She wanted to go to
church and wore a complete matching glorious linen.
Everyone at church took note. Nobody had shown
up in anything that swank since the Doubleday wedding. I was tired just thinking about her.

That same season, Peter brought his old Aunt
Minnie who had been in a wheelchair for thirty
years. She was a good sport when her chair wouldn't
clear the door. I was a good sport to take the doors
down. But we all knew that once in with Aunt Min
didn't solve any problems.

I was the only other female that weekend, so I got
Aunt Min in the tub, and Aunt Min out of the tub,
and Aunt Min slightly loaded to bed, and, I kept
thinking hopefully, I would soon get Aunt Min out
of my life.

The final blow—and what triggered my hate for
the whole scene—was when the McDuffs arrived
from Marlboro country. I had said it was okay last
February when the snow was on the ground.

"We just want to come up to the big city. Can we
stay in your barn when you're not there?"

The McDuffs, I might add, had King Ranch kind
of money and could have bought the Waldorf Towers.
But they hated to spend money.

"Fine," I said. "Sure."

Finally that dreaded letter arrived in June. The

McDuffs and brood were on their way. They were looking forward to seeing me. I wasn't looking forward to seeing them.

"I can't even go up, Pete. With that crowd there's no room for me and Clovis."

"Well, tell them to clear out by Friday," Pete said. It was his turn to just sit and bake.

They did not leave by Friday. Milly called and said she was sure that I didn't care. It was so much better for Bill and the kids to start back on the following Monday rather than hit weekend traffic.

I hinted about the city heat and Peter and Clovis and how much I wanted to get to the country.

Bill McDuff was a generous guy. He opened his big Marlboro heart and my door. "Why, for the love of heaven, why don't you and your guy come up here? One of the kids can sleep on the floor. Pete can have the couch."

It takes a lot of straws to do it. But this was it. Snapsville. I had had Versailles. I was going to come down out of that mountain once and for all and save my money for my old age which, hopefully, I could spend like Aunt Min, slightly tipsy.

XIV

I thought it would pass. But it didn't. The commuting weekends. The neighbors. The storm windows. The screens. The lawn. The moles. The birds and the bills. My terrace was splitting, the retaining wall was crumbling, the trees were dying, and the weeds were doing just fine.

The emotional strain of always trying to get something done was just too big. If it wasn't the terrace cracking, it was the paint peeling. If I had the couch covered, it made the chairs look dirty. The curtains should be replaced, but the shutter man didn't like casement windows. Someone threw a log in the fire and broke the andiron. The thought of finding a welder in Old Gosling to fix it was a bore. The sliding doors were off the track, and every time someone came and stayed, the screens fell off. Irving, an Irish wolfhound, had put his paw through the biggest screen I owned and my bill was $46. I only had a $50 deductible. Just having the place painted was more than I'd eventually get on my old-age check for the entire year. Who needed it all? Not I, old phoebeeeeeeee, not I.

I had just read of a businessman who had turned his home into a museum for a tax advantage. I considered the possibilities for the barn. But he had paintings. The closest thing I had to a Renoir was the framed bill for the artesian well. The rest of my art treasures were all hidden and would hardly entice anyone to pay the dollar entrance fee. I couldn't imagine them saying, "My what a stunning septic tank."

I thought of just leaving the barn to Old Gosling as a zoo for wild beasts in their native habitat. God knows I had enough rats, snakes, moles, cinch bugs, chipmunks, starlings, and carpenter ants to stock a zoo. But with my luck, the town assessor would double my taxes. She did every time I cut the lawn. No wonder the Hendersons fared so well.

Whether I liked it or not, Old Gosling was expanding. The sleepy little New England hamlet nestled in the heart of rough Connecticut country was maturing into a full-fledged town. Each week brought a further threat of citification as shopping centers sprang up, it seemed, overnight. There were now nine gas stations instead of three, and one even stayed open on Sunday night. And the Old Gosling *Press* bulged from four to twelve pages. As rumors for an expanded Route 6 reached me, I knew the future of the barn. It would be in the middle of a cloverleaf, and Clovis' life would be in danger.

No more petitions, no more complaints to the cops about guitars, no more bills for court hearings to keep progress at bay. I would chuck the place and get it over with.

"Who needs this?" I said to Peter.

"You do. It's your outlet."

"I'm going to take up karate."

"Oh, you love the place and you know it."

"No, I don't. I hate it, and I'm sick of it, and I work too hard, and I will die in the poorhouse at the rate I'm going. I'd have to have a counterfeiting machine to live here full-time."

"Well, you don't have to do everything at once," said Peter.

"If I don't, some damned law will be invented that won't let me. No, I've had it."

I stuck to my word, the hell with it. I got hold of Mr. Peabody, a real-estate man. Ma Henderson had gone off in a cloud of dust in her tin lizzie. She was now in the Green Pastures smoking a celestial cigar —and probably buying up clouds cheap that she would sell to me for a lot of bucks when I joined her.

"I'm going back to town to live," I said. "Back where the trees have to fight to live and don't just loll around waiting for a free lunch."

"Well, I might be able to find someone who would want to live in a place like this," said Mr. Peabody.

I couldn't help noticing his patronizing note about "a place like this."

"A place like what?" I asked belligerently.

"Well, now, ma'am, you know what I mean. It's just not typical. For instance, you have a mighty terrace, but no garage. It's a bahn!" He was very New England and a barn was a "bahn."

"I know it's a barn, but do you think you can sell it?"

"Oh, I do believe so, but it might take time!"

The following Saturday, Mr. Peabody phoned bright and early to tell me that a middle-aged couple was interested and wanted to see the place. They would bring their ancient mother, and, hopefully, their ancient capital. The old lady loved to garden, and would it be okay if they came in the morning to see how much dew was out?

I assured him that it was fine, just fine. I had a lunch date at Old Gosling Inn, and if I wasn't there after the dew count, he should just go in. The door would be open.

When I arrived home, there was a terse note to call Mr. Peabody the second I arrived.

"Did you sell it?" I asked hopefully.

"Nope, had a little trouble at your place."

"What kind of trouble? For heaven's sake, did someone fall?"

"Nope, nothing of that kind." He sounded peeved. More peeved than depressed.

"What happened?"

"I was showing the lady the bedroom and the dressing room, and everything seemed to please her, and it was so peaceful and quiet until I slid the door of the shower."

I knew what was coming.

"Well, you know, now in all the time I had been coming over to your place and showing it, I never seen no dog. I didn't even know you had one until I slid back the door of that shower. That big hairless feller you got stood up and yawned."

"Frightened the lady?"

"Well, I'd hardly say that. She likened to have a fit, she did."

"Oh, dear."

"Got to be frank, miss, it give me quite a turn, too."

"That did it, huh?"

"That lady flew out of that house, and no money in the world would get her back in. I thought she was going to crack wide open."

"Oh, dear."

"What kind of a dog is that anyway? I never saw anything like it."

"It's a tick-free sheepdog."

"Well, it's sure something to look at."

I told Mr. Peabody that I was going away for a month, and that he could go as low as one price and as high as he could get, but I wanted him to get rid of it in that month, come what may.

"Well, hope you take that dog with you."

"Oh, yes, she'll stay in town."

"To tell you the truth, miss, I've gotten to like the place since I've been showing it. Got a lot of charm."

"Why don't you buy it?"

"Sure would like to."

"Oh, you'll find someone."

"Yes, I'm sure we will. By the way, next time if you come up, before you go on your trip, I'd like to go over it with you once more. There are a few questions everyone asks that I don't know the answers to."

"Okay," I agreed, "the sooner we do it, the better."

I agreed to meet him the Saturday of the next weekend, as the following Monday I was going to leave.

Clovis and I drove up the Saw Mill River Parkway on a beautiful sunny fall afternoon. The Hudson, when we got a peek of it, was deep blue, the sky was deep blue, not a cloud, the sun was warm. The air bliss. An occasional whiff of burning leaves wafted across my nostrils: a nostalgic smell. I would always think of Mama in her "garbage and leaf" cremation sweater. It was a discard of Papa's which came to just above her knees, the sleeves folded back several times. The pockets sagged with nuts she carried for her squirrels, and clipping shears, and wire for propping chrysanthemums.

I simply didn't have what Mama had when it came to house and garden. I would never have that kind of home in my life with the kettle singing, fresh-cut flowers everywhere, little piles of burning leaves. What the devil, I thought, you tried. Old Gosling isn't for you. You're a city slicker. Face it, you tried for five years and what did it get you? I whistled a lot and I couldn't have been happier.

"You sure did an interesting job with your bahn," said Mr. Peabody when I picked him up.

Flattery wasn't going to get me this time.

"I have never seen a bahn like it in all my days."

Oh, well, he couldn't be *too* insincere. After all, if he didn't sell it, he didn't get his commission.

"One couple I showed it to wanted to put blinds up, and I thought that was a shame. I said so, too."

"Well, you're right. It would spoil the whole view," I added indignantly. How dare anyone put up blinds in the big living-room windows!

When we came up the road, lo and behold, the Hendersons had gone. I knew they were going to move when Ma died, but I hadn't been up there and had missed the taking down of the flag and the old tire swing in the tree.

"Their place is for sale, too. I'm handling that one, too. Tried to get a feller to buy yours and theirs. It would return the property to its natural state."

"That's a wreck, the Henderson place. They were one of the seven thousand reasons I wanted out."

"Well, they're gone now."

"It would cost a fortune to fix that up."

"Oh, I don't know. A person with some imagination would know what to do."

Ha, ha, I thought. Forget it! I fell for that line already.

"There was no reason why Orville couldn't have painted the place."

"Guess Orville didn't have much money."

"He had enough to subsidize the Italian-Swiss Colony Wine Company," I added.

"Guess Orville had a problem."

"Mr. Peabody, Orville was the problem."

"Don't want too much for the place."

"I don't care what they want for it. I know what they got it for."

He knew full well what had happened, and his eyes twinkled. "Maybe you could snap it up and make it an even bargain now."

I ignored him. One swindle in my life was enough.

When we arrived, Mr. Peabody got out his list and we went over the place. After he left, I walked about in the late Connecticut sunshine.

There was my garden, all gold and russet. My little copper beech still alive and struggling. "By heavens, I never thought you'd make it," I said, patting it and waiting a second to see if it died.

My Jesus Saves Rock was turning to gray amethyst, and a whole covey of the prettiest birds I ever saw was sitting on my lawn and on branches of the trees.

"Fakers! You're just props."

The birches were white-gold. All the Mrs. Firenzas and Bruno Schneiders and Else Runings and Dandy Sandys and moles and partridges were suddenly there, a batch of glorious giggling memories. Was this really the end of Old Gosling? Yes!

I had poured so much cement and me into the place, of course I'd miss it once in a while. Especially, I laughed, on the first of the month when the glass-front envelopes come.

I knew all about this place. Its weaknesses, its bad points. It was *my* house. If I spent money on it foolishly, it wasn't the barn's fault. It was my choice. Like a sugar daddy, I had spoiled my monstrous little girl.

"Hey, there," shouted Mr. Peabody, "I came back. I thought since you were just out today, you should take a look at the Hendersons' place. Just to know about selling yours and how it could affect you."

He wasn't kidding me one whit, but then, too, it was no joke to have Hendersons for neighbors. And the shape their house was in!

I had seen only the kitchen and the boat room. I had never been upstairs. Except for the Henderson color sense, it was pretty, actually, and each bedroom had a fireplace.

"Someone could put in a new bathroom and paint it a pretty color and you'd have a nice house."

"Mr. Peabody, I don't need another house in my life. I've got one I'm trying to get rid of."

"Well, now, you could rent a house like this fast here. People coming in getting jobs with Benrus and Perkins and places like them don't know if they're going to stay or not. Real market for picking up a nice dollah. And," he underlined, "you can have the kind of neighbors you want. And don't forget you can keep that piece of road property zoned the right way. So as you could protect the bahn."

All good points, but what did I care! Since I was trying to chuck the palace, who needed the game-keeper's house? Not this Lady Chatterley. (Especially with no gamekeeper.) But, then, on the other hand, a sly thought did enter my head: if I could make some money out of that property . . .

"Did you know there was an apple orchard up the hill?" Mr. Peabody asked.

"No," I answered.

He pointed it out to me in the golden-green light.

"A whole apple orchard?" I asked greedily.

"Yep, a whole little beauty of an orchard. Over two hundred trees."

We walked up past the house, up a steep hill to the orchard. It was simply not fair in a soft October sunset. I looked down at my barn. I remembered that half-green, half-yellow mess that Ma Henderson had showed me. And now I sighed at its simple beauty. Nostalgically. It was *me*. What had started out as a weekend lark away from the city had turned into a real house. More than that, this house was my home. *My* home. So what if it was a lump, an expensive lush! I was in love with it. I was hooked. I belonged to the House Generation. It wouldn't have been any different had I bought the all-linoleum house of the Cranwells or The Mouse House or the log cabin on Never Find It Lake. I would have done the same things to them that I had done to the barn. Mama had made her mark on me, regardless. I wanted a house in the country, in the air. I wanted a yard. I wanted to be away from where "it" was. I wanted to burn leaves. It was just a question of time till I wrinkled up and wore a garbage sweater.

My Jesus Saves Rock had turned black marble now, and there sat Clovis on her hill surveying it. I looked over at the old farmhouse. Wouldn't it be a shame to wreck it? I could see it now all rented and snug. A curl of smoke like Green Flower Farm coming out of the chimney. I didn't let myself see that the flashing on the chimney stack would be the first thing that had to be done.

"And see here—*I* didn't even know this—there's a whole row of wild-cherry and plum trees. This really was a farm, once, you know."

I had to hold on to the apple tree to have the strength not to say what I wanted to say. I tried to think of myself in charge of cows and animals. A whole cloister of monks making honey and cheese. The only problem would be no monks. Just old pals getting the ice out for drinks and innumerable calls from Mrs. Firenza.

"Oh, let's go. I'm getting cold."

Mr. Peabody offered to buy me a drink at the Old Gosling Inn. It would be a farewell drink to autumn. He was the most poetic real-estate agent I had ever met.

As we drove down the road away from the barn and the farmhouse, I looked back. Like Lot's wife said, "Don't ever look back."

At the Inn I called Peter.

"You'll never guess what we're going to do."

"We're going to Europe on Monday on vacation."

"No, I have a better idea." I told him all.

"Mahvelous."

Well, the details of the purchase were simple enough. Just a down payment to hold it until I got to the bank. Mr. Peabody was pleased as punch. He was a great Swamp Yankee just like all the rest. Instead of selling my place to someone else, he had sold me the house next door.

"But, Clovis," I explained to her on the way back, "now you'll have a whole apple orchard to protect, so you had better get in shape. And maybe I'll buy some sheep." That would be a shock to her, I'll tell you. She could barely keep *me* in her line of vision. (What would she do with a herd?)

There wasn't any point in talking to her; she had already gone to sleep, dreaming of fires and future naps. Her great gray dust-mop ears were filling out again, and they did perk up a bit as I started to sing.

> Oh, give me two homes,
> Where the Swamp Yankees roam,
> Where the deer and the antelope prey;
> Where seldom is heard
> An encouraging word
> And the bills keep on coming all day.

818.54
Tr
Trahey, Jane
Pecked to death by goslings

DATE DUE			
JE 11 '71			
JY 19 '71			
AG 5 '71			
AG 11 '71			
AG 20 '71			
1-10-73			
31 Aug			

GAYLORD · PRINTED IN U.S.A.